Write,
Right,
Rite!

Write,
Right,
Rite!

Gerald R. Oglan

Wayne State University

Boston   New York   San Francisco
Mexico City   Montreal   Toronto   London   Madrid   Munich   Paris
Hong Kong   Singapore   Tokyo   Cape Town   Sydney

Series editor: *Aurora Martínez-Ramos*
Editorial assistant: *Beth Slater*
Senior marketing manager: *Elizabeth Fogarty*
Manufacturing buyer: *Andrew Turso*
Cover designer: *Suzanne Harbison*
Production coordinator: *Pat Torelli Publishing Services*
Editorial-production service: *Stratford Publishing Services, Inc.*
Electronic composition: *Stratford Publishing Services, Inc.*

For related titles and support materials, visit our online catalog at www.ablongman.com.

Library of Congress Cataloging-in-Publication Data
Oglan, Gerald R.
  Write, right, rite! / Gerald R. Oglan.
    p. cm.
  ISBN 0-205-34424-0
  1. English language--Rhetoric--Study and teaching. 2. Report writing--Study and teaching (Higher) I. Title.

PE1404 .O33 2002
808'.042'0711--dc21   2002026040

Printed in the United States of America
10 9 8 7 6 5 4 3 2 1   06 05 04 03 02

To Maureen, Nadia, and Jarrod

Contents

Preface

Why a Book about Writing?

It seemed as though I was always questioning the teaching of writing during my twenty years as a classroom teacher. This book is intended to share strategies on teaching writing in hopes that new conversations will emerge among teachers and parents who work with students in school and at home. Over the last five years I have worked with teachers in developing an approach that will support the school curriculum while at the same time developing a student's competency as a writer, with particular attention to the revision and editing of text. The information and strategies presented here have been field-tested with teachers and classrooms from grades 1 through 8. This book represents a continuation of my work with teachers (*Writing Sense*, 1997) and with parents (*Parents, Learning, and Whole Language Classrooms*, 1997; *Parent to Parent: Our Children, Their Literacy*, 2001), who constantly push my thinking.

Theoretically, the book views the development of an open model of teaching writing. An open model examines what goes on in the minds of students when they write, acknowledges the social elements that facilitate writing, and views oral language as a conduit between what goes on in the mind and what gets written on paper. An open model emphasizes the construction of meaning, drawing on the individual's prior knowledge, experience, background, and social context. In an open model of writing three curricular areas are addressed: word study, personal writing, and writing for publication.

In Figure 1, circles are highlighted using broken or dotted lines. The broken line represents movement between the three areas. For instance, what is done in word study can support personal writing, and vice versa. Writing for publication, which involves revision and editing, can enhance a student's knowledge of grammatical structures as well as vocabulary. The following descriptions represent definitions of the three curricular areas.

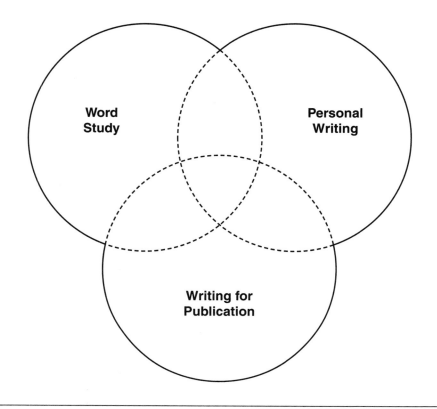

FIGURE 1   *WRITING CURRICULUM FRAMEWORK*

Word Study

Word study refers to strategies students use while exploring the nature of sounds and letters and their relationships. Some common strategies include crossword puzzles, word searches, word webs, word grids, word families, theme words, and word power, to name a few. Learning words is enhanced when the brain can attach "felt meaning" (Caine & Caine, 1991). Felt meaning places words in a context. For instance, when students work on a crossword puzzle, there may be a theme (sports, movies, and so on) related to the words. Contextualizing words through a theme is more engaging because it places the words within a topic or subject.

A second consideration when learning new words is "chunking." Chunking, or finding certain patterns in words, is what the brain does well. For instance, "sign" can be found in a variety of words, such as *design, resign,* and *assign,* all with the same articulation pattern. Articulation shifts when the pattern is found in words such as *signature* and *signal*. When students "study" words, they make connections to sounds and visual features of words.

Personal Writing

Personal writing is defined as a time when students have the opportunity to write for pleasure and personal meaning. The most common example of personal writing is journal writing, where students are invited to write about a range of experiences. Other examples of personal writing include diaries, personal anecdotes, messages, informal notes, and so on. Personal writing allows students to express themselves without worrying about accuracy. Personal writing supports reflection. Reflection requires students to think about what they learned during a math lesson, science experiment, or writing experience. Through written reflection students express what they learned, what they are still thinking about, or in what new directions they want to take their learning. Writing is a way to record reflections at any given time on any given subject. Making thoughts explicit through writing can provide an evaluation tool for the teacher. When students write in a learning log, they create a personal benchmark for their own learning. This benchmark serves as "baseline data," to which students return throughout the year for reflecting on what they have learned and comparing their thinking to others about topics and issues. In comparing their thinking to others, children must first be able to listen to other children. Graves (1994) found that children first externalize their listening ability—that is, they concentrate on what others say before "going underground" to listen to themselves. Going underground requires that students have opportunities to reflect. Because this form of writing is personal, sensitive, and intimate, teachers should respect the risks students take and should not grade or write comments that may deter them from sharing their thoughts.

Writing for Publication

Writing for publication is a time when students are expected to publish a piece of writing. Publications include various genres such as a school or class newsletter, a portfolio, a letter to a politician or local newspaper. The focus of writing is on content and accuracy. Writing for publication presented in this book highlights the differences between a closed model of writing and an open model. Teachers want students who can take an idea and develop it into a published piece of writing. However, a closed approach does not encourage or support revision and editing—the processes that authors and writers experience when they write for publication. Revision and editing are the key to the publishing process and should be taught starting in first grade. Chapter 4 outlines a process teachers can use to implement revision and editing in their writing programs.

Pulling Your Program Together

Word study, personal writing, and writing for publication are not implemented separately. All three are addressed through writing programs, and all three of these curricular areas provide students with experiences and opportunities to develop depth of knowledge about words, sounds, and letters, as well as writing and publishing. Chapter 6 outlines a genre approach to writing, highlighting eight major genres and fifty-two subgenres, or formats: personal (diaries, journals, invitations, postcards), report and inform (time lines, interviews, scrapbooks), instruct and explain (recipes, menus, game rules), poetry (rhymes, patterned poems, free verse), traditional literature (hero tales, fables, tall tales), word play (riddles, jokes, comic strips), narrative (scripts, fiction), and opinion and persuasion (brochures, advice columns, posters/slogans).

The Cueing Systems and Writing

Learning to write involves four cueing systems: semantic (prior knowledge), syntactic (grammar and word order), graphophonemic (sounds/letters and their relationships), and the pragmatic (knowledge about social situations). All four cueing systems work together during writing and are enhanced through word study, personal writing, and writing for publication. Teachers need a working knowledge of the cueing systems before they implement their writing programs. For instance, understanding the semantic system of language is key to implementing revision. Syntax and graphophonemic systems come into play during conventional editing and deal with the surface-level features of text (spelling, punctuation, and grammar). Knowing the functions of the cueing systems and their relationship to writing is the key to establishing a writing program using an open model.

Communication Systems and Writing

The communication systems include reading, writing, speaking, listening, viewing, and visual representing. Writing is one communication system used to express meaning and word awareness, and spelling develops when it is embedded in writing experiences. Teachers support students in this process by establishing a classroom environment that encourages students to use what they know about sounds letters and their relationships in a variety of writing experiences. Communication systems support classrooms that view writing as a social process, encourage risk taking, understand the role of functional spellings, trust students while they write and spell, offer choice and ownership, establish a framework for writing, and follow a child's lead.

Writing As a Social Process

Individuals become literate, not from the formal instruction they receive, but what they read and who they read and write with.

—Frank Smith, 1985

As students speak and listen, they share their ideas and insights about language and clarify their thinking. Their insights support the social nature of language learning.

Risk Taking and Functional Spelling

It's a damn poor mind indeed which can't think of at least two ways to spell any word.

—Andrew Jackson

From the beginning of a school year, students must feel comfortable using functional spellings. Functional spellings are words children use that are not spelled in conventional form. The term "functional" is used because the spellings serve a purpose in their writing: Encouraging students to use functional spellings allows a teacher to determine what they know about language. Students who take risks by using functional spellings can predict and generate hypotheses about language, testing what they already know and generating new patterns.

Trust

> *For children to achieve this active involvement in their own learning, it is important to find ways of enabling them to share in the responsibility of deciding what tasks to undertake.*
>
> —Gordon Wells, 1986

Through trust and relaxation of external control, teachers and students are free to negotiate and engage in experiences from which learning will inevitably follow. Once children know the teacher trusts them, they take control of their own learning.

Choice and Ownership

> *My spelling is Wobbly. It's good spelling but it wobbles and the letters get in all of the wrong places.*
>
> —A. A. Milne

Choice is an integral part of the language arts curriculum (Harste, Woodward, & Burke, 1984). Choice comes into play when children are free to make decisions about the text they produce, creating a feeling of ownership. When children have a feeling of ownership for the tasks in which they engage, teachers find that their relationships with children change (Wells, 1986). Children no longer need close supervision every moment of the day, because they know what has to be done. They use their time productively, usually asking for assistance only when all other sources prove to be inadequate.

Prior Knowledge

> *In the process of constructing their own knowledge, spelling is not viewed as a separate subject to be learned, but is part of the literacy learning experience.*
>
> —G. R. Oglan, 1992

If teachers believe that children come to school knowing a great deal about language through previous experience, then there can be no advantaged or disadvantaged learners. Students are creators of their own knowledge through writing and reading about events that they know something about.

Following the Student's Lead

> *In following the student's lead as often as we ask them to follow ours, we are showing our interest in several aspects of what children have to share—topics of interest in their life outside of school, resources and artifacts that they provide, and happenings we didn't plan on.*
> —Bobbi Fisher and Pat Coderio, 1994

Students have all sorts of ideas and projects they want to work on. When teachers allow students time to explore their interests through speaking, writing, reading, listening, viewing, and representing, language learning is enhanced. By following the student's lead, a teacher is in a better position to offer suggestions, ask questions, and act as a collaborator in the process.

The Curriculum

> *As our alphabet now stands, the bad spelling, or what is called so, is generally the best, as conforming to the sounds, letters and the words.*
> —Benjamin Franklin

Good curriculums support a philosophy that empowers students. Students are in control of their learning through the choices they make about reading, writing, speaking, listening, viewing, and representing. Spelling is embedded in everything they do. Students are encouraged to explore relationships and patterns within words, at all times, and across all subjects and conversations. Spelling growth occurs over time as each student makes connections about sounds, letters, and their relationships.

How This Book Is Set Up

Two models of learning to write will be examined: a closed model, in which teachers view writing as a step-by-step, sequential process; and an open model, in which teachers view writing as a meaning-making process. Chapter 1 sets the theoretical framework for examining differences between open and closed models. Chapter 2 looks at the communication systems (reading, writing, speaking, listening, viewing, and representing) and cueing systems of language (semantics, syntax, graphophonemics, and pragmatics). Chapter 3 examines the developmental nature of learning to write and spell. Common spelling strategies are identified and examined within the context of student writing. Chapter 4 looks at writing for publication, with an emphasis on revision and editing. The key to writing for publication is to shift the responsibility for revision and editing from a teacher-directed approach to a student-centered approach. Chapter 5 examines word study as it relates to the graphophonemic system (sounds, letters, and their relationships) and why it is important to provide students with opportunities to "study" words. Chapter 6 outlines a genre approach to writing, defining genres and explaining how formats can be used in the writing program. Chapter 7 offers recommendations on implementing the spelling curriculum framework.

Each chapter ends with a story about teachers and students who are implementing word study, personal writing, and writing for publication in their classrooms. The stories act as a lens for viewing how other teachers are using the strategies and writing frameworks presented in this book. It is my hope that you will learn from their experiences.

Acknowledgments

I actually started writing this book during my years as a classroom teacher. I was always looking for new strategies to use with my students and consequently found myself trying a variety of activities to get my students to write. Part of my dilemma was that I had never really written and published anything myself. As a result, I viewed writing as a task-completion activity. During my twenty years in public education, I had an opportunity to work with many talented teachers. However, it wasn't until I published my first book that I really felt I understood the complexity of writing. I began working with classroom teachers during my four years as an elementary language-arts consultant. During this time, I started looking at writing and publication, with a focus on revision and editing. I continued my research in this area when I left public education and moved into a university setting. After almost ten years of field-testing my ideas, I believe I am closer to helping classroom teachers meet the writing needs of their students.

This book is a culmination of my work to date. Well after this book is published, work will need to continue to address the needs of teachers, students, and parents as they relate to writing. Having spent twelve years teaching students with learning disabilities I felt strongly about including them in this book. I learned a great deal from them, and I know the frustration they feel when they are expected to write. I also included sections for ESL (English as a second language) students. Spending time with teachers and students in Detroit and Hamtramck, Michigan, taught me a great deal about the writing needs of ESL students.

I would like to thank Fred Borowski, principal at the University Public School (UPS) in Detroit. UPS is a middle school that provided me with an opportunity to work with many talented teachers. In particular, I would like to thank the following teachers for their contributions to this book: Willie Williams, Anita Ricks-Bates, Rhonda Calloway, and Simone L. Ecola. They had the courage and took risks to implement strategies and philosophies highlighted in this book. Two other teachers I am grateful to: Ann Marie Mahlmeister of Holbrook Elementary School in Hamtramck,

Michigan, who saw what could be done with her second-grade students. The majority of her students are identified as ESL and are showing promise in their writing. Rick Scott, my Canadian friend and colleague from Windsor, Ontario, is one of those rare individuals who enjoys teaching second- and third-grade students. After attending one of my workshops, he implemented a publication program with his third-graders. When I first visited his classroom, he said, "Gerry, it doesn't get any better than this." He continues to refine and fine-tune his program, based on his own learning. (Now, if he only could play golf as well as he can teach!)

Where there are teachers there are students. Thanks to the students and their parents who allowed me to use their work in this book: Maha Najmidin Al-Shaweyh, Holbrook Elementary; Jasmine Porter, University Public School; Ashley Harris, University Public School; Janelle Moore, University Public School; and Daniel Turlescu, St. Angela School.

My appreciation also goes to the following reviewers for their helpful comments on the manuscript: Charlotte Black, California State University, San Bernadino; Barbara Franczyk, University of Wisconsin–Milwaukee; Kathryn Leo-Nyquist, Champlain University; and Janelle Mathais, University of North Texas.

Finally, many thanks to all of the teachers and students in Canada and the United States who welcomed me into their classrooms over the last decade.

1

Models of Writing
Stepping Back, Looking Forward

During the last decade, I often asked teachers who have been involved in the writing process with their students, "How do you encourage children to use their growing understanding of written language to develop as authors when revising a text for publication?" The following are representative of the answers I received.

"I do most of the revision because my kids don't know how."

"I tried to get my kids to revise but they don't know what to look for."

"Only a few of the kids in my class are capable of revising and editing their work or others."

"My students rush through revision just to get done."

These answers indicate a closed model of revision. In such a model the teacher controls revision, making decisions for authors about their text. Many teachers were taught or trained in closed systems of learning, and therefore their classroom programs reflect these experiences. This is not intended to be judgmental toward teachers. I taught that way for years, experiencing the same frustrations with my own students. The approach advocated in this book views revision in an open model.

Consider the following scenarios based on the experiences of two fourth-grade teachers.

Scenario 1

The fourth-grade teacher looked at Meredith's writing sample and asked, "Where is the rough draft of this piece that I wrote on?"

Meredith walked over to the classroom file of writing folders and rummaged through her file until she found the first draft where her teacher had written suggestions relating to revising parts of the text. "Mrs. Smith, here is my draft. I'm sorry that I forgot to staple my draft to this piece. Do you think that I am ready to publish it?"

"Hmmm," she hummed as her eyes skimmed the paper checking for a beginning sentence that introduced the topic, details supporting the body of the text and a concluding sentence that summarized the story. Completing a revision checklist she smiled into Meredith's eyes and said, "You're ready to publish!"

Meredith bounced back to the publishing center in the classroom and stapled the revision checklist to the rough draft, rewrote the final copy which was then filed into her writing portfolio. (Oglan & Donnelley, 1999)

Scenario 2

A group of fourth-grade students have signed up for an author's circle and are listening to one member read his story while the teacher is conducting a writing conference with another group of students and the rest of the class is working on individual pieces of writing.

"Yes, but *why* did you choose to use the word 'said' again?"

"Because the boy said those words."

"I know that the boy said, 'I'll tell you who did it.' But, you know, did he scream it, whisper it, or cry it?"

"Oh yeah. Do we still have that chart where we listed all those words, I mean synonyms, for said?" His eyes skimmed the room and he stopped by the door. He contemplated the words on the list and finally turned to his classmate, who had followed him to the door, and stated, "I still don't know which word is the best choice. Thanks to you I know that's it's not 'said'! I mean, man, I'm on my third draft and I still don't think it's finished."

"Yeah. Why don't you go look in one of those *Fractured Fairy Tale* books and maybe that'll help you decide." (Oglan & Donnelley, 1999)

The two scenarios are indicative of classrooms where teachers' beliefs about writing influence how revision is handled. Many teachers rely on their own experiences with writing or on professional development training. The problem comes when they attempt to implement revision and editing with their students. The strategies suggested in this book are a result of working with teachers who have given up on getting their students to revise and edit their work. Working with classroom teachers helped me understand that revision of text has been a source of frustration for well-intentioned teachers whose only desire is for their students to be able to revise their own work. So why are teachers struggling with this issue?

Writing: Process or Product?

The two scenarios above clearly demonstrate the dichotomy between two classrooms that value and invite writing. Both classrooms describe learning environments that encourage children to view themselves as writers. Yet their revision processes look and sound very different. What is so striking is that in one classroom (Scenario 2) children were clearly in charge of listening and asking questions that might make a difference in their classmate's piece. The questioning strategies used to help an author consider more detailed language was accepted as part of the writing process. As they talked with one another about a piece of writing, they naturally accessed the tools they created to facilitate the writing process. Charts that hung in the classroom contained lists of synonyms, character traits, and questions about setting and plot, and the books in the classroom library were familiar to the children. Conversations prompted the use and reuse of these resources. Children also used each other as resources to assist the author in making critical decisions on word choice, topic, or illustration. So why was the teacher the source of revision in one classroom (Scenario 1) whereas students had ownership of revision in the other (Scenario 2)?

For the purpose of clarity, a distinction must be drawn between *revision* and *editing*. Revision deals with semantics of a text—the meaning and messages an author wants the reader to understand. In an open model, revision requires that the authors read their text to others, who provide feedback on parts or sections of the text that appear confusing and in need of clarification. Editing refers to changes an author makes to surface-level features of the text, including spelling, punctuation, and grammar. These are often referred to as the conventions of written language. In traditional closed-model classrooms editing is often viewed as the primary function of writing for publication, whereas in an open model, editing is viewed as only one part of the publication process, which can occur before, during, and after revision.

Revision: An Open-Model Perspective

In Scenario 2, revision and editing is viewed as a recursive process, in which the students revisit their texts to add details and deeper meaning (Harste, Short, & Burke, 1988). The boys continually shifted from sharing their views about a piece to uninterrupted reading and writing, as they searched for the phrase or word that would best fit the needs of that piece. Moving from discussion back to personal writing and reflection may vary, depending on the degree of importance and significance of each piece of writing. When students believe that revision is part of a process that is undertaken every time they write, they move away from a closed model of writing (write draft, teacher corrects, copy over) to an open model. Good writing, the kind that awakens your imagination, makes you cry, moves you to take action, or even shares interesting information, comes from writers who make informed predictions about revisions that best suit the purposes of that piece. Encouraging the use of a fluid process is what seems to make an important difference.

Classrooms that support the social nature of writing encourage students to take risks, resulting in writers who share their best thoughts with fellow writers. As a result, young authors push one another to publish their best thinking. Just as language operates as an open model, the process of revision supports a whole/part/whole model. One obvious difference empowering children as writers rests in the critical stance they adopt in order to provide truly meaningful feedback.

Revision: A Closed-Model Perspective

Revision is the search for text that may appear to a reader as confusing or in need of clarification. Sometimes the author may need help teasing out the essence of an idea. Students are expected to read their pieces to other students who are not familiar with the story for the purpose of receiving suggestions for consideration. The final decision to change or revise any part of a text is always the decision of the author. In my conversations with teachers, I learned that revision was not specifically taught. In fact, it was often assumed that revising a text for meaning was a skill students arrived with at the beginning of the school year. Demonstrating the process of revising a text in order to make a message more clearly understood for the reader was something teachers thought little about. Most teachers lumped revision (which deals with the meaning potential of the author's intended message) with conventional editing (which deals with surface-level features of text, such as punctuation, spelling, or grammar). The two are distinctly different. Atwell (1987) believes that asking students to edit before the content is set reflects misunderstanding of what writers do. Semantic revision must precede conventional editing, and most of the author's attention should be focused on semantic revisions. In many classrooms the opposite is true. That is, most teachers, in their desire to lump revision and editing together, place more emphasis on surface editing and spend less time (if any) on the semantics of the piece. Atwell agrees:

> Teachers and students who focus on editorial issues in early drafts are de-emphasizing information and disallowing the real possibility that revision will allow for changes of such magnitude that the final draft will be significantly different. (1987, p. 106)

Moving away from a closed model of revision and editing to an open model places more ownership and responsibility on the student and less on the teacher. To better understand the impact of these competing models on writing and the teaching of writing, they are framed within paradigm perspectives in the following section.

Open and Closed Models: A Paradigm Perspective

Teaching word study, personal writing, and writing for publication can be grounded in two paradigms, both of which are at the center of the debate over writing, and the successes and failures that teachers experience in their classrooms: the **empirical** (quantitative/positivist/closed-model) **paradigm** and the **interpretive** (qualitative/experiencialist/open-model) **paradigm**. A paradigm is defined as "a conceptual framework with a loosely connected set of ideas, values, and rules that govern the conduct of inquiry, the way in which data are interpreted, and the way the world may be viewed" (Shubert, 1986, p. 170). Zvric (1997) defines a paradigm as the lens through which the world is perceived by a person or group of persons. According to Shubert (1986), the empirical paradigm is orderly, sequentially driven, and how everything can be proved. This paradigm is in search of truth. Knowledge is transmitted hierarchically by experts (teachers) and is acquired by the masses (students). When knowledge is presented in the same way to a group of individuals, a closed model exists.

By contrast, an interpretive paradigm sees the world in the context of meaning, not truth. There can be multiple meanings and ways to communicate them in the context of cultures. Cultures can exist anywhere and are not limited to societies. Classrooms can be considered cultures (Zvric, 1997, p. 29). When personal meaning and prior knowledge are valued in learning experiences, an open model exists.

Closed Model's View of Language Development

The empirical paradigm has its roots in the behavioral model of teaching that originated in the late 1800s and continued through the late 1960s and early 1970s, when it shifted to a cognitive model. Figure 1.1 illustrates an empirical perspective of language learning and methodology.

In a closed model of language, learning is viewed as a part-to-whole method: Students are required to learn sounds and letters before moving to words and sentences. Information is presented in a sequence, and the learner has to master the concepts in each sequence before moving on to the next step. In a subject such as spelling, students are taught the rules that govern the use of sounds in words (i before e except after c, and so on), using words from their spelling textbook. Letters and sounds are highlighted in weekly lessons, reinforcing words where phonetic structures (e.g., "f" and "ph") are used. Grammatical structures (e.g., er, ur, or, ir) are also addressed through weekly lessons. Sentences take their forms from the words, and students are expected to write the weekly words in a sentence to show they have mastered how, when, and where to apply the grammatical and phonetic structures. On the weekly spelling test, the teacher dictates sentences to see if students can write and spell the words of the week.

Formal Context

A formal context exists when the teacher imposes what is to be learned and written about. For example, in reading, where basal readers are used

Belief/View	Methodology
View of language	Closed
View of context	Formal
Response to errors	Eliminate
Meaning found in	Text
Role of the learner	Passive
Motivation	Extrinsic

FIGURE 1.1   *CLOSED MODEL*

Source: From Gerald R. Oglan, *Parents, Learning, and Whole Language Classrooms.* Copyright © 1997 by the National Council of Teachers of English. Reprinted with permission.

exclusively, students learn the words in a story through drill and memorization, prior to reading the story. Once these words are mastered, students are expected to read stories in large groups. Students take turns reading aloud to their peers while the teacher listens for mispronounced words, immediately correcting the readers' errors and making sure they can pronounce the word before reading further. Students are given the topics of the stories they are to write about and, sometimes, the number of words they should use. By imposing what students are expected to learn, ownership of the activity is taken out of the hands, hearts, and minds of the students and placed in the overall control of teachers. There is little room for individual thinking, and students are expected to "conform" to their teacher's wishes.

Response to Errors

Errors are viewed as a student's failure to learn. By concentrating on eliminating errors, teachers make accuracy the focus for all activity. Students are evaluated on the number of correct responses and are given letter grades and percentages. Grades are often posted in the classroom for everyone to see. Perfection is the goal, regardless of the subject, and this is achieved mostly through memorization, drill, and repetition. The focus on perfection affects students' responses to tests and exams, causing stress and anxiety.

Meaning and Text

Meaning refers to what learners bring to a situation and how they interpret events based on prior knowledge. Meaning in an empirical paradigm is addressed through repeated exposure to text. For instance, objects are associated with words presented by adults. Repeated associations of objects with words form a bond (Harste, Woodward, & Burke, 1984). Practice and participation through repeated drill enhances the learning when the learner is aware of the success of each attempt at an answer. Students find meaning in the text, or, in many cases, in how the teacher interprets the text and word meanings. Evaluation and assessment are based on the teacher's perspective. Teachers rely on manuals and guides to help explain meaning. With text-driven meaning, little attention is given to individuality and prior knowledge of the learner. The authority in the classroom is the teacher and the texts and manuals he or she relies on to establish meaning.

Passive Learners

The learner's role in the empirical model is passive. Students are presented with the information, and learning is controlled by the teacher or classroom environment. Quiet rooms are considered productive and conducive to learning. Authority seems to dominate not only what is done, but when, by whom, and at what time. The old saw that "children should be seen and not heard" is the rule of thumb.

Motivation

Positive reinforcement is used to reward accuracy and good behavior in the classroom, a method of motivation advocated by B. F. Skinner. In 1954 Skinner developed a number of models based on the premise that immediate reinforcement is effective in influencing learning (Shephard & Regan, 1982). According to Skinner's theory, extrinsic motivation is based on rewards and punishments and forces the elimination of errors and controls unacceptable behavior.

Another method of motivation is grouping. Students are grouped according to grade and ability to compete. For instance, the "Jets" reading group is the fastest and its members among the first to finish their work, whereas the "Turtles" always need extra time to catch up.

Reflecting on the Closed-Model Perspective

The closed model is not a paradigm that encourages risk taking. Conformity is expected through the "factory model" of learning, so called because schools up to the late 1960s were modeled after industry where materials were mass-produced and flawless products were the goal; workers were expected to perform their jobs diligently and to be members of the status quo. In the classroom, speaking was limited to speeches and teacher-led discussions. The remainder of the time was quiet work time.

Open-Model View of Language Learning

The open model evolved from an interpretive paradigm, which emphasizes the role of the learner, as well as the classroom environment, in the learning process. Meaning is at the core of this paradigm. To connect meaning to the learning experience, an individual must draw upon a lifetime of knowledge, experience, and cognitive strategies. Therefore, another key to this paradigm is accepting prior knowledge that learners bring into the classroom (see Figure 1.2). Children come to school with a vast knowledge of language patterns. Much of this tacit knowledge is a direct result of the experiences that children have enjoyed before entering school. Parents, other family members, and peers have nurtured children's awareness of language. As oral language emerges, the role of the parent or caregiver is extremely important—not as instructor, but as facilitator—through discussion, play, and demonstration (Hall, 1987). In addition, before entering school, children are surrounded by print. Most children arrive at school knowing something about written language, how it works, and what it is used for (Hall, 1987). What children know—their life experiences—becomes a touchstone on which curriculum is made vital and ever alive (Harste, Woodward, & Burke, 1984). This is how learning is viewed in an open model.

Open Models

Because open models are based on a meaning model of learning that draws on previous learning experiences and the prior knowledge that an individual brings to any learning event, the interpretation of text in reading, of numbers in mathematics, and approaches to problem solving will differ among individuals in the class. Students may learn to solve mathematical problems using approaches and theories they have developed that are different from those used by others. Teachers create a positive environment by respecting the thinking and diversity that students bring into the classroom, and use this information as learning opportunities to teach their students about multiple ways of knowing. Teachers use questioning

Belief/View	Methodology
View of language	Open
View of context	Authentic
Response to errors	Errors seen as miscues
Meaning found in	Prior knowledge
Role of the learner	Transactive
Motivation	Intrinsic

FIGURE 1.2   *OPEN MODEL*

Source: From Gerald R. Oglan, *Parents, Learning, and Whole Language Classrooms.* Copyright © 1997 by the National Council of Teachers of English. Reprinted with permission.

strategies as one way to get to the source of their students' thinking and to encourage their active participation. Questioning is what stimulates our brains.

Authentic Context

Open models are neither student-centered nor teacher-driven; they are learner-focused. In this context, everyone in the classroom (including the principal, janitor, and any parent or adult who happens to enter the room) can be a voice of authority or an expert at something. When students are valued for their multiple ways of knowing, problem solving becomes a social process. Students are able to tap into the thinking potential of both their peers and the adults who surround them on a daily basis. As one parent discovered as she wrote her own family story, "People are naturally social beings. We do a lot of our learning when interacting with each other. We look to each other for assistance, answers to our questions, and solutions to our problems." Such an approach to learning can be encouraged in art, music, drama, and mathematics, as well as other areas.

Response to Errors

"Authentic," or open-model, writing experiences allow students to read, write, and explore language in areas that interest them. Errors are viewed as "miscues," a term first used by Kenneth Goodman (1967) to describe any departure the reader makes from the actual words of the text. Goodman cited two reasons for using the term. First, he wanted to recognize that departure from the words of the text is not always problematic or in error; and second, he wanted to emphasize how such departures indicate which language cueing model (syntax, semantics, graphophonemics, pragmatics) the reader is using (Weaver, 1988). Yetta Goodman (1989) viewed a child's miscues as an attempt at displaying knowledge about phonics while simultaneously using language. In so doing, the reader/writer uses a self-correcting process to follow the text.

When a child writes using previous experiences, conventional spellings increase because the child is rehearsing strategies involving words learned previously. Conventional spelling decreases when children experiment with new strategies because they attempt to spell more complex words in an unfamiliar context. Thus, a student's writing reflects substantial signs of growth through the functional (or "invented") spellings used. Rather than rehearsing words in isolation and being tested on memory and the ability to repeat back information, a child is supported as a participant in his or her own growth by teachers who understand that learning involves taking risks and constructing knowledge about language, not simply participating passively.

Children learn about language as they use it, and are influenced by the audiences for whom they are writing. Meaning is constructed when a child is allowed to use functional spelling when drafting stories, writing in journals, writing letters to pen pals, or writing dialogue. It has been wrongly assumed that unless the markings are conventional, they are not intentional (Whitin, Mills, & O'Keefe, 1990). Experiences are the key to language growth and involve the learner exploring and testing what he or she already knows about language. Thus the environment and the learner come together to generate new experiences and to enhance the potential for language growth. A learner who plays with language is allowed the opportunity to make new connections.

Meaning and Text

Meaning is multimodal and context-dependent; verbal symbols and signs—numbers, letters, and words—and nonverbal symbols and signs—drawings, art forms, and mimes—have meaning potential, depending on the context presented and the previous experiences of the individuals using them. This can be illustrated using the number 25. When working with parents, I put this number on an overhead projector and ask them to tell me what this number means. The following are some of the answers I usually receive:

- Age
- Anniversary
- 5×5
- One-fourth of 100
- 5 squared
- 25 ones
- 2 tens and 5 ones
- 100 divided by 4
- Distance
- A measurement of some kind

The answer to the question depends on the context in which it is used. In this case, the above answers represent a range of possible contexts in which the number 25 could have meaning. Harste, Woodward, and Burke (1984) highlight the idea of context-dependent meaning using the golden arches of McDonald's. In studying the language development of young children, they found that symbols establish meaning. When children saw the

McDonald's sign, they exclaimed "hamburger," not reading the words but constructing meaning using the symbol. This supports the theory that pictures and visual clues play a role in predicting meaning. The meaning potential of signs and symbols has it roots in the field of semiotics, the study of sign models.

Transactional Learners

Whenever the learning environment and the learner come together, a bilateral effect should occur. Dewey (1938) identified this effect as a *transaction*. When students transact with oral and written language, changes occur in what they know about language. One transaction should lead to another; thus, language learning is never static but is in a constant state of flux. Children learn about sounds, letters, and their relationships through their use of language. The role of the adult in this process is to facilitate the development of language by asking questions, not giving answers, thereby providing students opportunities for thinking, responding, and asking questions. When teachers ask questions they infringe on comfort zones, but questions don't threaten: They guide students into asking and answering their own questions about language. Vygotsky (1978) identified growth as the "zone of proximal development." That zone is the distance between a student's actual development level, as determined by independent problem solving, and the area of potential growth, as determined through problem solving under adult guidance. "What a child can do with the assistance of others might be in some sense even more indicative of their mental development than what they can do alone" (Vygotsky, 1978, p. 85).

Motivation

In an open model students take ownership of their learning. Students are made to feel valued and part of the community of learners in the classroom. As in all communities, there are expectations of its members, including the responsibility for ensuring that the learning climate is supportive and free of sarcasm and put-down. Learning is viewed as a social process in which helping others, listening, speaking, reading, and writing are ways of negotiating meaning. Risk taking is viewed not as something to fear but as a strategy to learn new ways of knowing. There is no pressure, and stress is limited. As a result, students, teachers, and adults become engaged in a process of self-discovery. This process challenges their thinking, and keeps them interested enough to keep moving ahead. It is a relaxed state of learning that enhances the learning potential of all students.

Reflecting on the Interpretive Open Model

Teachers' beliefs about how children learn have a direct influence on the classroom environment. Just as we expect our students to read, write, and expand their awareness, so must we as professionals do the same. Students learn to develop responsibility for their writing when they see the adults in their world modeling and demonstrating what real writers do in their daily lives. Teachers, in particular, have a responsibility to evaluate ideas and proposals on their merit and not just passively accept them on the grounds of authority, real or presumed (Allen & Van Buren, 1971). An open model offers teachers an opportunity to learn about writing with their students. It places teachers in a position to be part of the writing experiences of their students and not stand outside as a voice of authority. They become another voice students can rely on when they need support or guidance.

Summary

Understanding the differences between open and closed models may explain why revision and editing in writing has become a struggle for teachers. It may also shed new light on why students have difficulty performing on state and provincial standardized writing tests. Mandated state and provincial testing has incorporated performance-based assessments. These types of assessments require students to produce a piece of writing by taking it through the writing process. Students must demonstrate their skills by producing a draft that has been revised and edited for publication. The process explained in the following chapters has been field-tested with students in grades 1 through 8. It is my hope that readers will find information that can help students and teachers develop as authors.

TEACHER STORY • *Think, Talk, Write*

Ann Marie Mahlmeister
Grade 2, Holbrook Elementary School
Hamtramck, Michigan

I wanted to help my second-grade students write more in their journals. Our school district has a lot of ESL students and writing has been a problem. For instance, in my class I have five Bengali students, sixteen Arabic students, six African American students, and one Polish student. I decided to try "Think, Talk, Write." On Friday, I asked the students to think about what they would be doing on the weekend. I gave them one minute to think about the events. Following the minute, I told them to get a partner and tell that partner what they thought they would do on the weekend. Again, I gave them each a minute to share. The purpose of allowing only one minute is to keep them focused on thinking and talking. Once they each had a minute to share, I then invited them to write in their journals and make "predictions" about what they thought they might do on the weekend. Figure 1.3 shows what one of the students wrote on Friday.

On Monday, I repeated the process, allowing them a minute to think about what they had actually done on the weekend and then share that with one other person. Then I asked them to look at the prediction they had written on Friday and describe whether they had actually done what they had predicted on Friday, and if not, then describe why. Figure 1.4 shows what the student wrote on Monday.

It was obvious that Monday's journal used more text than did Friday's. In fact, on Friday the student used 33 words, 4, or 12 percent, of

I will clean my room wath T.V. clean my bogbag go out side go to my kasints house and then Nade and her sister is going to come to my house and riyt.

FIGURE 1.3 *SECOND-GRADE FRIDAY JOURNAL*

Nada came to my house and we played techer and then we wath PokéMon and then we wint back to play techer and then I was the techer and then Nade was the kide we did some wirk even her sisther played with us even my sisther played and we have so math fun.

FIGURE 1.4   *SECOND-GRADE MONDAY JOURNAL ENTRY*

which were functional and 29, or 88 percent, of which were conventional. On Monday, the student wrote 54 words, 9, or 16 percent, of which were functional, and 46, or 84 percent, of which were conventional. "Think, Talk, Write" acted as a framework for students to make predictions on Friday and then on Monday, confirm or reject their predictions by providing more information. With some of my ESL students, who may have limited writing skills, I have them do a "Think, Talk, Draw" on both days. This gives them an opportunity to share their pictures, using oral language to express their predictions and confirmations.

2

Systems at Work

It is important to set the framework for how cueing systems and communication systems transact. Transacting refers to how the systems are used by learners to communicate. A brief explanation of the two systems follows.

Communication Systems

The communication systems discussed here are reading, writing, speaking, listening, viewing, and representing. Students use some or all of these communication systems throughout the day. Some students may have a preference for one or another. Special populations, such as ESL/bilingual children and children with learning disabilities, gravitate to certain communication systems because of their unique learning styles. For instance, ESL students may use drawings to communicate knowledge about their cultures and how they learn. Viewing and representing become the preferred communication systems employed by these students. As they learn about the English language, they gradually move toward writing as the preferred communication system. While writing, students may access a "word wall," word charts, or a list of thematic words to help them spell and expand their vocabulary. In doing so, students use viewing to help them during writing.

   Reading is the process whereby readers construct meaning from print. Readers transact with the text for the purpose of securing information and/or enjoyment. Transactions, according to Rosenblatt (1978) occur when a reader and a text come together. The reader's prior knowledge determines how the text is interpreted. Goodman (1996) notes that our brains play a key role in the reading process by setting up expectations and instructing our eyes to glide over the surface of the print, and using that input to make sense of print. The brain is so good at making sense out of print that it will even try to attach "sense" to "nonsense" (see cueing systems for examples).

Reading is more than word identification. It is a complex process involving prior knowledge, experience with text, and the brain's ability to use information to make sense and bring meaning to the text. Reading is not restricted to print. Young children read wordless picture books and have conversations about the pictures as a story unfolds. Young children rely on viewing, speaking, and listening, as well as their prior knowledge, to make meaning out of the reading process.

Writing is a process whereby writers select, develop, arrange, and record ideas in a variety of forms, for a variety of purposes and audiences. Writing is a tool for communication, critical thinking, and self-expression. All writers use language to represent ideas, experiences, social relationships, and social and personal understandings (Goodman, 1996). Young writers represent their ideas and thoughts in a number of ways. For instance, they may use "scribble writing"—marking the page but not using letters—and pictures to help project their meaning. As they mature, their writing reflects their knowledge of sounds, letters, and their relationships. Initially, they may use more consonants in their writing because consonants carry more meaning than do vowels, making it easier to communicate their messages. As they get older, children learn how to use their knowledge about genres to enhance their writing. For instance, the language used for writing a postcard differs from the language used when writing an invitation or a friendly letter. Interest also drives writing, so a student who likes sports and wants to write about his or her favorite hockey player may produce a more sophisticated piece of writing than if he or she is asked to write about something unfamiliar.

Speaking and **listening** are ways of communicating ideas to different audiences in a variety of situations and forms. From the time children are born they use speaking and listening to communicate. Parents identify the sounds children make to determine their needs. Crying usually indicates hunger, a need for a diaper change, discomfort after eating, or just fussiness. Noncrying sounds, such as cooing, gurgles, sighs, and grunts indicate that a child is happy and satisfied (Oglan & Elcombe, 2001). Children recognize their mother's voice and image and respond by smiling or laughing. When children start to walk and talk, parents help them develop oral language patterns by demonstrating the correct use of the English language. For instance, a young child may say, "Mommy goed to the store." The parent may model the correct form of the language and reply, "That is right, Mommy went to the store." Like reading and writing, speaking and listening cannot be separated because both systems impact on one another. By the time children enter formal schooling they have considerable knowledge about letters and sounds. As they progress through elementary school, speaking and listening continue to develop through classroom experiences.

Viewing involves the interpretation of and response to visual media, such as film, television, art, photos, illustrations, videos, and computer technology. Viewing develops a student's ability to examine content and form. For young children, viewing may take the form of looking at picture books, or listening to a story and viewing the pictures for the purpose of discussing the story. Viewing is used to make sense out of the environment. When we "read" the environment, we pay attention to where things belong and may notice when things are out of order. As a communication system, viewing is something we rely on to take in information for a variety of functions, such as reading, writing, and observing an event or experience.

Representing involves the use of materials to construct personal meaning. For instance, a child may use Legos to make a structure and describe it as a person, place, or thing. Children in preschool and kindergarten represent their thinking while playing in sand or water, or with finger paints, plasticine, or large and small blocks. Structures and other creations represent castles, forts, homes, cities, animals, and so on. Young children love to talk about their creations, often telling stories. Older children may be asked to make a collage to represent the abstract thinking of a story. Graphic organizers, such as semantic maps, storyboards, sketches, and diagrams are used to represent a concept, or the meaning of a story.

People use many of the communication systems to express themselves, depending on the purpose or experience. For instance, during guided reading a teacher may have students read a story and discuss what they have read. In this case, the communication systems employed are reading, speaking, and listening. Use of communication systems will vary, depending on the activity or strategy a teacher uses, and they are supported through the cueing systems.

Cueing Systems

Communication systems work closely with cueing systems: semantics, syntax, pragmatics, and graphophonemics. **Semantics**, constructing meaning, involves prior knowledge. Words have specific meaning when they are embedded in a context. **Pragmatics** refers to the way individuals use language in social settings within a specific context. This includes meaning but also takes into consideration social and cultural context. **Syntax** is the grammar of language that contributes to the ongoing flow of language. It takes into account such things as word order, tense, connecting phrases, and gender. **Graphophonemics** refers to the relationship between letters (grapheme) and sounds (phoneme). Sound refers to oral language, sometimes called the **phonological system**, and letters refer to written language, or the **orthographic system**. The relationship between the two is known as **phonics**. The following story demonstrates how the cueing systems function.

Cordanic

Cordanic is an emerent grof with many fribs; it granks from corite, an olg which cargs like lange. Corite grinkles several other tarances, which garkers excarp by glarcking the cortie and starping it in tranker-clarped storbs. The tarances starp a chark which is exasperated with worters, branking a slorp. This slorp is garped through several coruscus, finally frasting a pragety, blick-ant crankle: coranda. Coranda is a cargurt, grinkling corandic and borigen. The corandic is narcerated from the borigen by means of loracity. Thus garkers finally thrap a glick, bracht, glupous, grapant, cordanic, which granks in many sarps. (Weaver, 2002)

This story posseses all of the features of the English language. It has syntax (grammar), graphophonemics (letter-sound relationships), and some words that the reader can identify. However, the struggle exists when the reader tries to use the semantic and pragmatic systems. The reader cannot establish meaning or draw upon prior knowledge to understand context because the language is not familiar. Students experience the same frustration when they write in genres that are not familiar to them. ESL students and students with learning disabilities (LD) experience similar problems with the cueing systems and need to expand their prior knowledge.

Such developmentally special populations initially move across the continuum from right to left (see Figure 2.1) because their strengths are in viewing, representing, listening, and speaking. In terms of perceptual strengths, many of them are visual, tactile, and kinesthetic, meaning they work best when they can see information to be learned and use touch and body awareness. Viewing (visual) and representing (using tactile/kinesthetic modalities) support their learning styles. The focus for these students in reading and writing should be centered around strategies that incorporate their communication strengths. "Regular" students (students without such challenges) move across the continuum from left to right,

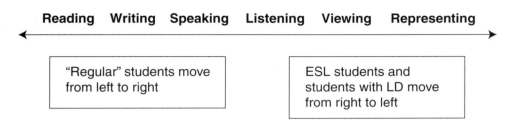

FIGURE 2.1 *COMMUNICATION SYSTEMS*

their strengths being in reading and writing. Speaking and listening are common to both groups and should be used as a focus in the development of other communication systems. All learners are placed on the continuum and are viewed as having strengths in some aspect of the communication/cueing systems. Teachers, students, and parents should strive to help individuals move back and forth across the continuum.

Systems at Work

Teachers are encouraged to think about programs for their classrooms and then place the strategies they use on a chart. This gives them an assessment tool for systems as well as a profile of their classroom curriculums. For a demonstration of how communication and cueing can work together, see Figure 2.2, which highlights strategies classroom teachers use as part of their programs and curriculums.

By identifying strategies and communication/cueing systems, teachers create a profile of programs. In order to address all of the systems, teachers need a range of strategies to meet the needs of their students. Figure 2.3 illustrates how all of the systems work together when a person is communicating. Two key features of this systems model are **personal knowing** and **social knowing**. Personal knowing is intuitive knowledge about a range of topics or subjects. Social knowing is knowledge gained in conversation and in other social settings.

Systems and Curriculum Planning

Taking time to place strategies on the systems chart serves as a curricular planning tool. Once completed, the chart helps teachers analyze the gaps,

Strategy	Communication	Cueing Systems
Literature circles	Speaking, listening	Semantics, pragmatics
Venn diagram	Reading, representing, viewing, speaking	Semantics, pragmatics
Reader's theater	Reading, representing, viewing, listening, speaking	Syntax, semantics, pragmatics, graphophonemics
Personal journals	Writing	Pragmatics, semantics, syntax, graphophonemics
Word wall	Reading, writing, representing, viewing	Graphophonemics
Writing for publication	Reading, writing, speaking, listening	Graphophonemics, syntax, semantics, pragmatics
Picture books	Viewing, representing, reading, speaking, listening	Semantics, pragmatics
Note taking	Viewing, representing, reading, listening, writing, speaking	Semantics, pragmatics, syntax, graphophonemics
Oral/written projects	Reading, writing, speaking, listening, viewing, representing	Semantics, syntax, pragmatics, graphophonemics

FIGURE 2.2   *SYSTEMS AT WORK*

make informed curricular decisions, and identify emerging patterns. For instance, a teacher may find a number of strategies that address all of the cueing systems, but they are all grouped (at the top) under writing and reading. A teacher would then look for strategies to help students develop skills in listening, viewing, representing, and speaking. At the same time, a teacher whose students are not keeping up with the classroom programs may find that a heavy emphasis on reading and writing may negatively affect the student's assessment.

New teachers find the chart a convenient way to handle the enormous amount of information in their first few years of teaching. By keeping track of the strategies they use on a daily basis, as well as any new strategies they may encounter through professional development and in-service training, teachers identify gaps in their programs. Assessment strategies can be added to the chart to form an overall profile of the program. For instance a teacher,

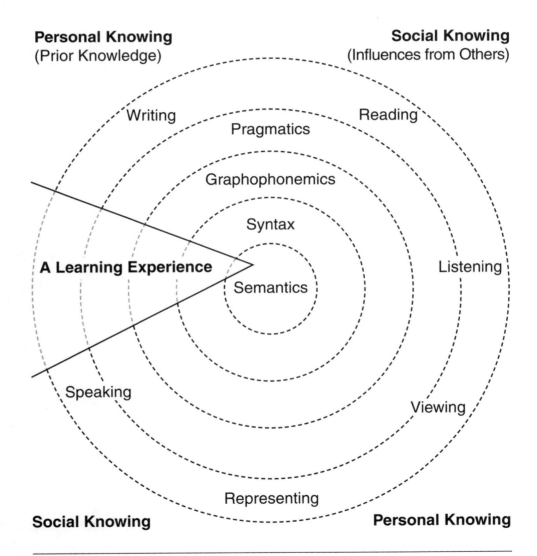

FIGURE 2.3   *SYSTEMS MODEL*

Source: Adapted from J.C. Harste, K.G. Short, and C. Burke, *Creating Classrooms for Authors*. New York: Routledge, Chapman and Hall, 1988.

using running records (an assessment tool based on the Reading Recovery Program) or rubrics for writing assessment can add these to the chart. Informal assessments, such as spelling dictations and cloze strategies (identifying missing letters in words, or missing phrases in sentences) can also be added. Each year teachers build their programs and make curriculum decisions based on the communication and cueing systems. Understanding how students develop as writers and spellers is the key to planning curriculum.

Systems and Assessment

During reporting periods, the systems chart is used to assess students' strengths within the communication systems while highlighting the cueing systems. Teachers are encouraged to look for patterns in their students. For instance, a student who likes to draw, take part in plays, and work at a computer is developing skills in listening, viewing, representing, and speaking; but this student may need help with reading and writing when it's time for writing for publication. On the other hand, a student who likes to just read and write and does not utilize other communication systems needs to be taught strategies to expand their communication potential. Patterns of communication may be more distinct with ESL students, for example. Students who are learning to speak English need experiences that help them conceptualize relationships between their first language and English. Many of their initial experiences may be social in nature, where they attempt to learn meaning (semantics) and context (pragmatics) through speaking and listening.

Summary

Understanding how the communication and cueing systems function in the classroom is the key to addressing the learning needs of all students in your classroom. As you observe your students, try to identify those who have a preference for certain communication systems. For instance, all classrooms have students who like to build, draw, and make things. Initially, these students may write best when they can use these skills in their work. Chapter 6 examines genres of writing and how to incorporate them into your writing program. They provide teachers with a wide range of writing strategies to help address the communication needs of students. Students who have a preference for certain communication systems may gravitate to certain genres. For example, creating postcards can strengthen skills or lead to the creation of comic strips. Understanding the developmental nature of learning to spell and establishing a writing program to deal with spelling development will be covered in Chapter 3.

TEACHER STORY • *Wish Lists*

Rick Scott
Grade 3, St. Angela Catholic School
Windsor, Ontario

To start my writing program I like to get the students thinking about semantics when they write. To accomplish this, I introduce the students to short stories that are in need of revision. I create the stories based on the writing patterns in the students' journals. I let them work in groups and I introduce the idea of "wishing." When they read the text, they look for words that are confusing or in need of clarification.

```
One rainy cloudy and awful day 2 girls went
to this large place. They playeded all kinds
of games. At four o'clock their parents
picked them up. They went to a beautiful
Italian restaurant to eat. The family got
home at 10:00 and went right to bed. They
had an exhausting day.
```

The students are then asked to write a wish (or wishes) that would provide more detail to the story.

I wish to know who the two girls are!
I wish to know what games they played.
I wish to know what food the two girls ate.

Once students have written their wishes they are asked to revise and rewrite the story incorporating their wishes.

One rainy, cloudy and awful day two girls,
Cristi and this Caroline went to this large place.
They also play all kinds of games like "lazer tag" and
sorry. At four o'clock their parents picked them up.
Then they went to a beautiful Italian resteront
to eat brocoly soup and pizza. The family got home
at 10:00pm and went right to bed. They had a
exhausting day.

It takes a week for the students to feel comfortable with making wishes and revising the text. In the second week I introduce editing. I supply the children with plastic hats to use while they edit work for spelling, grammar, and punctuation.

3

Writing and Spelling

Today spelling is often the focus of debates and conversations between parents, teachers, and administrators. It seems as though everyone has an opinion about how spelling should be taught, its value, and the role it plays in writing. The debate is not new. It has been around for hundreds of years. The purpose of this chapter is twofold. First, it is important for readers to have a sense of the history of spelling and its impact on contemporary issues. Second, examining the developmental nature of learning to spell and how writers use what they know about language is important in our understanding of the complexity of the writing process.

Historical Perspective of Spelling

The printing press was invented in 1476, and William Caxton (1422–1491) of London was one the first printers who attempted to standardize the English language. Because of the many dialects spoken in England during this time, Caxton was forced to make some arbitrary decisions about how to print certain words. For example, he printed "sayled" for sailed and "frenshe" for French. Because of the limitations of the early printing press, Caxton could not print a clear letter "u" so he changed it to an "o" and created such words as "come," "wonder," and "love" (Phenix & Scott-Dunne, 1991).

In 1604, Robert Cawdray produced a dictionary of 120 pages called the *Table Alphabetical*. He wrote it for "ladies and any other unskillful persons." In 1755, Samuel Johnson published a dictionary in which he defined some 40,000 words with accompanying analogies and quotations. His purpose for writing the dictionary was to enable future generations to read, enjoy, and interpret Shakespeare's writings.

In 1802, Noah Webster completed his first dictionary of American English. Like Caxton, he made arbitrary decisions about certain spellings. For example, he changed waggon to wagon, robbin to robin, colour to color and musick to music. In making such decisions, Webster created confusion about spelling. The established rule stated that in words that had more than one syllable, where a consonant followed a short vowel, the consonant had to be doubled. Webster employed an "exception to the rule." Little did Webster, and others who followed him, realize the impact their decisions would have on the learning and teaching of spelling in years to come. Today, spelling is considered correct or incorrect based on arbitrary, and sometimes illogical, decisions made by one early printer and two dictionary writers (Phenix & Scott-Dunne, 1991).

While Webster and others were writing dictionaries, the American curriculum experienced a dramatic change. Textbooks became the standardizing influence on the curriculum. In Chicago, between 1855 and 1864, all students in the Chicago school system were put into graded classrooms, and a course of study was established (Kliebard, 1989). By the turn of the century the American curriculum was divided into two groups.

Spelling: Caught or Taught?

As early as 1897, when the teaching of spelling was a universal practice, the possibility of it being "caught" (like a common cold) was considered by Joseph Mayer Rice (1897). Rice wrote an article titled "The Futility of the Spelling Grind," suggesting that with statistical evidence he could prove that systematic phonics was not the only method of teaching spelling and that spelling was learned implicitly. Rice's article was supported by Corman (1902), who agreed that spelling could be approached through activities such as reading and written work. Rice and Corman's work marked a departure from a drill-and-rote memorization approach, leaving people wondering whether spelling was caught rather than taught through a direct and systematic phonics approach. The notion that spelling could be caught rather than taught was soon challenged by researchers determined to prove that systematic phonics was the most effective approach to the teaching of spelling. Wallin (1910) provided statistical evidence indicating that spelling was indeed taught and not caught as Rice and Corman had suggested. So the controversy had come to rest, and throughout the twentieth century spelling would continue to be the focus of research.

Traditional Education, Progressive Education, and Spelling

From the late 1800s to the early 1930s progressive educators believed children learned best when the materials to be learned met some recognized need, not when learning was through memorizing meaningless materials. The child should have many contacts with people, places, objects, books, and other printed materials; the school should be concerned with the physical, social, emotional, and mental development of the child (Shephard & Regan, 1982).

Traditional educators opposed the progressive movement. They believed in measurement, tight standards, and training children to take on adult roles. This was the focus of their curriculum. Traditional education was driven by a "scientific" curriculum in which two closely related movements in psychology came together. One was the development of a psychological theory, and the other was cognitive testing to evaluate learning. The calibration of intelligence into minute units (IQ points) was to affect profoundly the curriculum of American schools (Kliebard, 1989). Curriculums were developed to address variations in IQ levels. Students with higher IQs were presumed to be capable of more difficult work. The work of behavioral psychologists such as Pavlov, Thorndike, Skinner, Watson, Wolpe, Becker, and Estes, along with developmental psychologists such as Piaget, Erikson, Allport, Kohlberf, and Loevinger, had a profound effect on education from 1930 to the late 1960s. Learning, teaching, curriculum, and evaluation were viewed as drill and repetition supported by extrinsic rewards. A majority of the first seventy-three Association of Educational Research Awards (AERA) presented between 1915 and 1989 came from educational psychology, or from testing, and statistics allied to educational psychology (Gage, 1989, p.9).

Spelling and Contemporary Issues

In the last decade, considerable debate has focused on the teaching of spelling. In some cases, states have chosen to mandate the teaching of spelling using traditional closed model approaches whereas others support holistic open models in developing their curriculums. This book does not suggest that the strategies recommended in the teaching of spelling will work all of the time, in every classroom, with every student. But it does support a curriculum that is grounded in the open model discussed in Chapter 1, which requires teachers to have a working knowledge of how children think and learn and how the classroom environment can support this process.

Writing and Spelling Framework

One of the questions most frequently asked by parents is, "Why does my child get a perfect score on her weekly spelling quiz, but spell the same words wrong when she writes?" Parents who ask this usually were taught that good spellers should be good writers. The fact is that spelling and writing are different cognitive processes that support the systems of language. A closed model of spelling, referred to as a "part-to-whole" model, assumes a "mastery" approach to spelling. In a mastery approach, students are expected to learn sounds that accompany the letters of the alphabet, apply these sounds and letters to words, write sentences using the words, and eventually write stories. This closed model assumes that all children progress at the same rate and therefore must master each level of spelling development before moving on. The problem with this model is that learning a prescribed number of words each week and being tested for mastery is not consistent with what real writers do when they write. In an open model, sounds, letters, and their relationships are best learned while writing in a variety of genres. Students learn words by using them on a regular basis while writing for real audiences, with a specific purpose in mind.

The Developmental Nature of Spelling

From the moment children start to write, they view writing as a way to communicate their thoughts and feelings. They learn by watching adults write letters, notes, grocery lists, and so on, all examples of how writing can be used. Parents love to describe their children's first attempts at writing. They may involve anything, from writing on driveways and walls in the house to writing books and creating drawings. Many children begin with nonstandard writing (see Figure 3.1). Some people refer to this as "scribble writing." I prefer the term "nonstandard writing" because the marks on the page represent a child's thinking and attempts at com-

FIGURE 3.1   *NONSTANDARD WRITING*

municating their thoughts on paper. Although it may not appear conventional on the surface, the marks on the page represent personal meaning to the child.

When working with young children it is important to acknowledge their attempts at writing and not to downplay it by calling it "scribble writing." This tells a child you value their attempts at writing. Ask children to read their stories and they will go on and on, using speaking to connect meaning to the marks on the page. Newman (1984) identified four concepts to use when looking at a child's writing: intention, organization, experimentation, and orchestration.

In Figures 3.1 and 3.2, the child wants to communicate. He or she knows that marks on the page are used by the adults in their world and attempts to model this through his or her writing. Both figures show organization. That is, they are written from left to right, top to bottom. Figure 3.2 is a grocery list, and it is clear that this child knows that lists are written in a vertical format. Even at a young age, this writer is using knowledge about genres. In both figures we see the writers experimenting with language. In Figure 3.1, we can see attempts at writing letters such as "n" "h" and "i." In Figure 3.2, the child is not afraid to take risks by using what he or she knows about sounds and letters to represent the words and their meanings. Risk taking is a big part of experimenting, and both children feel comfortable in their attempts. Writing involves the ability to manage a number of cueing systems at once, incorporating semantics, syntax, graphophonemics, and pragmatics.

When young children start to write they primarily use consonants. Why? Because most consonants have a one-to-one sound/letter correspondence and are therefore more predictable than vowels. For example, the word "cat" has three letters and three distinct sounds. Children start to use spaces to separate words and write in a left-to-right pattern. When students enter school their writing and spelling take on specific characteristics and patterns, which will be discussed in detail in the following section.

Characteristics and Patterns of Spellers

This section discusses three types of spellers commonly found in classrooms. The purpose in identifying them is not to label students but rather to point out that a "range" of spellers exist in any learning environment. Through this awareness, teachers are in a better position to help students who may be struggling with spelling. For instance, a student who may be considered a reluctant speller in one context may be viewed as an independent speller in another. The key is to understand the comfort level of

FIGURE 3.2 *YOUNG CHILD'S GROCERY LIST*

the student and move from there to the cueing systems in writing and spelling (see Chapter 2). Reluctant, developing, and independent spellers represent a range of spellers. Figure 3.3 highlights characteristics of each.

The sliding scale in Figure 3.3 demonstrates how a learner can move from being a reluctant speller to an independent speller. Students need not be "stuck" in one spot on the scale. The purpose of the sliding scale is to identify the range of spellers in any given class and then help students develop an understanding about spelling through word study, personal writing, and writing for publication.

Context determines how well a learner can spell. Reluctant spellers like to write about things they are familiar with using "safe language," so their writing will reflect a high degree of accuracy. Students are intimidated by words they cannot spell and as a result use vocabulary they know how to spell, which keeps them within their "comfort zones." Students are not usually willing to "stretch" their knowledge about sounds, letters, and their relationships. Therefore, it is important to support and encourage reluctant spellers to move from writing about topics they are comfortable with to less-familiar topics of interest.

Sliding Scale

←————————————————————————————→

Reluctant Spellers

- Use high-frequency words (words they know how to spell)
- Focus on accuracy
- Do not take risks
- Prefer to work alone
- May generate very little text

Developing Spellers

- Use functional spellings
- Are often not willing to take risks when spelling
- Feel comfortable asking for help
- Use textual sources to confirm conventional spellings
- Work with other students
- Rely mostly on sounding-out strategies

Independent Spellers

- Feel comfortable using functional spellings
- Use a variety of textual sources to confirm spellings
- Ask questions about spelling
- Are willing to help others
- Display a sense of self-confidence
- Self-edit written work
- Are usually called on by others for assistance

FIGURE 3.3   *CHARACTERISTICS OF THREE TYPES OF SPELLERS*

When students move out of their comfort zone they begin to develop as spellers. They move away from relying on safe language to unfamiliar and complex text. Teachers can encourage students by providing opportunities and learning experiences that nudge students into experimenting with more complex language. The word patterns and functional spellings they produce are common and predictable. Functional spellings are often referred to as "invented" spelling. I prefer the term "functional" because it implies a purpose—a placeholder for the conventional form. Because some children perceive themselves as "poor" spellers, they do not care about spelling and therefore do not view it as important. These children pose a challenge because they may find more comfort writing about personal experiences using language they know and thus avoid revision and editing. They may need additional support and encouragement in the form of a writing partner, a parent volunteer, or from textual sources, such as dictionaries, word walls, and word charts. Without these kinds of support, their spelling may not improve.

The following is a list of the most common spelling strategies used by students as they write and spell (Oglan, 1992).

Spelling Strategies

1. **Letter name**
   Each letter of a word sounds like the name of the letter. Vowels are usually absent (e.g., first/frst, letter/ltr).

2. **Spelling as it sounds**
   Students rely on the sounds they hear that are close to the actual sound (e.g., uncle/uncul, feather/fethir).

3. **Placeholder**
   When spelling words with vowels, students will replace one vowel with another that is similar in sound (e,g., went/wont, video/vedio).

4. **Representation**
   Students sometimes know that a vowel is needed but insert a random vowel (e.g., misery/maziry, sometime/semtim).

5. **Overgeneralization**
   When students discover a new structure, such as the silent e at the end of a word, they use it repeatedly (e.g., won/wone, from/frome).

6. **Transpositonal**
   Words are spelled using all of the correct letters, but the letters are in the wrong order (e.g., tried/tride, watch/wacht).

7. **Visual**

   Words have a visual likeness to the conventional form (e.g., school/scool, teacher/techer).

8. **Articulation**

   Vowels and consonants are close in sound and are usually used interchangeably (e.g., combat/kombat, graphics/grafics).

9. **One letter misses**

   The word is close to the conventional form with the exception of one letter (e.g., snowed/snowd, waiting/wating).

10. **Multiple strategies**

    Students use a combination of the strategies (e.g., neighborhood/nebrhode, retirement/ritearment).

To understand how these strategies look in a piece of writing, see Figure 3.4, which was taken from a fourth-grade student's personal journal.

I wont to my Aunts cottage
wath my Consaunts We
had to win tocans by doing
things. I cam in second. I wan
fiv dolers and 50$ and stacers
and a teshrt. frist plas got
a teshrt and a candal.

FIGURE 3.4   *FOURTH-GRADE JOURNAL WRITING*

Strategies at Work

In this example, the student used a **placeholder** strategy (replacing a vowel with one that is close in sound) in went (wont), with (wath), and won (wan). In cousins (cousants), T-shirt (teshrt), and candle (candal) the student spelled them the way they **sounded**, and in the word "first" (frst), he used a **letter-name** strategy. In spelling came (cam), five (fiv), and place (plas), two possible strategies are present: **spelling as it sounds** and **visual**. It is more likely the student used a visual strategy, given the visual similarities between the functional spelling and the conventional form. (Students often move from relying on sounding-out strategies to visual likeness as they develop awareness of conventional spellings.) These three examples suggest that the student is on the verge of spelling these words conventionally. In the word "place" (plas), an **articulation** strategy is represented by the use of "s" for "c". An **articulation** strategy was also used on stickers (stacers) and tokens (tocans) where "c," "ck," and "k" sound alike.

The strategies used in this example suggest that this student is a developing speller. He knew a great deal about spelling. His functional spellings reflect his knowledge about sound-letter relationships. He is a risk taker, as evidenced by the number of functional words he uses. In response, his teacher could then do lessons in silent e words, and word families, or word webs, that deal with letters that sound the same, such as "c" and "s," as well as "c," "ck," and "k."

Unlike developing spellers, reluctant spellers have a tendency to use words they know how to spell. Why? Because they believe that good writers spell everything correctly. They do not like to take risks in their writing and enjoy the safety of using only words they know how to spell. In Figure 3.5 we see this eighth-grade student had very few misspelled words.

Although the page is full, a close examination of the spelling shows the student used only 3 functional spellings in a total of 197 words. In this case, the teacher told the students that their stories had to be a page in length. When limits are placed on writing, reluctant spellers view the length of the text as a priority and therefore use words they know how to spell so that they can complete the assignment and not have to worry about correcting spelling. One parent told me that one night she noticed her child (who was in Grade 8) counting the words to a story he had written:

> "Why are you counting the words?"
> "Because the teacher said we had to have five hundred in our story or lose marks."
> "So how many do you have?"

When I was in grade eight I had Mr Mueller as
a teacher he was a very good one too. I had fun
the first three weeks until my soccerball got roofed
I was upset. But I can also kick hard but I wrote
a story it was all about a line moving Well here it is.

One day all of my friends were fighting I walked
up and asked them what it was all about. Next thing
I know I was on the ground flat with a whole bunch
of blood all over me. Some people rushed me into the
hospital my neck was stiff my leg was broken my arm
was broken and blood was rushing out of me.

The docter's shaved ives into me. Then I
through up I was very mad I wanted to go home
They did an oporation and it took them 47 hours
and 27 minute 32 seconds and 13 micro seconds. I
left on December of 1992 then I was crumpled.

But I am still alive.

The End.

FIGURE 3.5   *EIGHTH-GRADE RELUCTANT SPELLER*

"Four-hundred and ninety-seven."
"What are you going to do?"
"Oh, I will add a couple of 'ands' and a 'the' to get me to five hundred."

Limitations and expectations have a place in writing, but for reluctant
writers they can be counterproductive to the development of writing.

Developing spellers may look like poor spellers and writers on the surface (see Figure 3.6).

In this piece, we can see that he knows how to write a letter by the opening, "Mom," and the closing, "Love, Jarrod." He uses contractions, "I'am," and capitalizes the first-person pronoun, "I." He used **spelling as it sounds** strategies for brought (brot), wrote (rot), finger (feger), and note (not). When he spelled signed (singed) on his first attempt, he used a **transpositional** spelling strategy, and when he wrote "sign" on his second attempt he spelled it correctly. When children spell words with all of the correct letters present but in the wrong order, it indicates that the child is about to internalize the correct spelling. On the word tomorrow (tomoro) he knew how to spell the word "to" and added "moro"; but if he had included the letter "w" his spelling would have been only one letter away from being correct.

When children spell words with double consonants the only way for them to know the correct spelling is to internalize it. This comes with seeing it many times, which is why we emphasize the importance of reading to and with children. On left (lift) he used a **placeholder** strategy because the short "e" is close in sound to the short "i." The spelling of the word

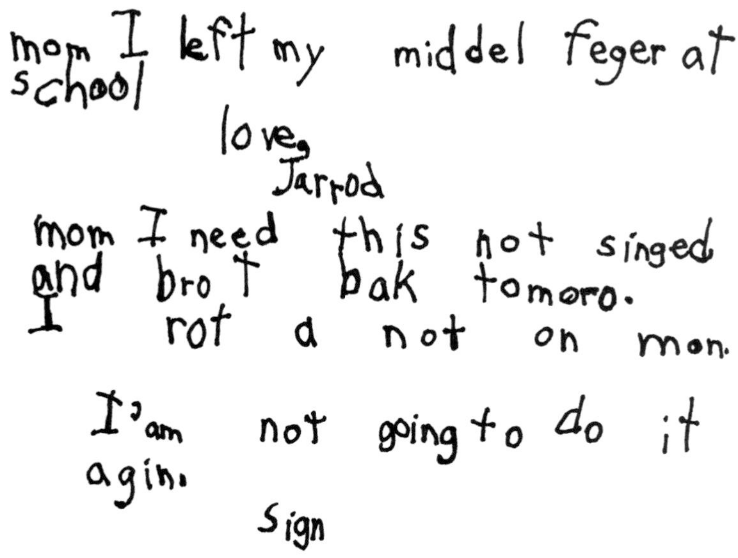

mom I left my middel feger at
school
        love,
            Jarrod
mom I need this not singed
and brot bak tomoro.
I rot a not on mon.

I'am not going to do it
agin.
        Sign

FIGURE 3.6 *DEVELOPING SPELLER*

"agin" probably shows some influence of the Southern dialect, because this student was living in South Carolina at the time.

Independent spellers feel comfortable using functional spelling (see Figure 3.7) and are often called upon by others to help with editing and revision. They are not afraid to ask questions or ask others for help. In this example, we see a variety of functional spellings. The text flows and the author's voice is present. The story has a beginning, a middle, and an end.

The student used a total of 108 words with 12 (11 percent) functional spellings and 96 (89 percent) conventional spellings. What observations

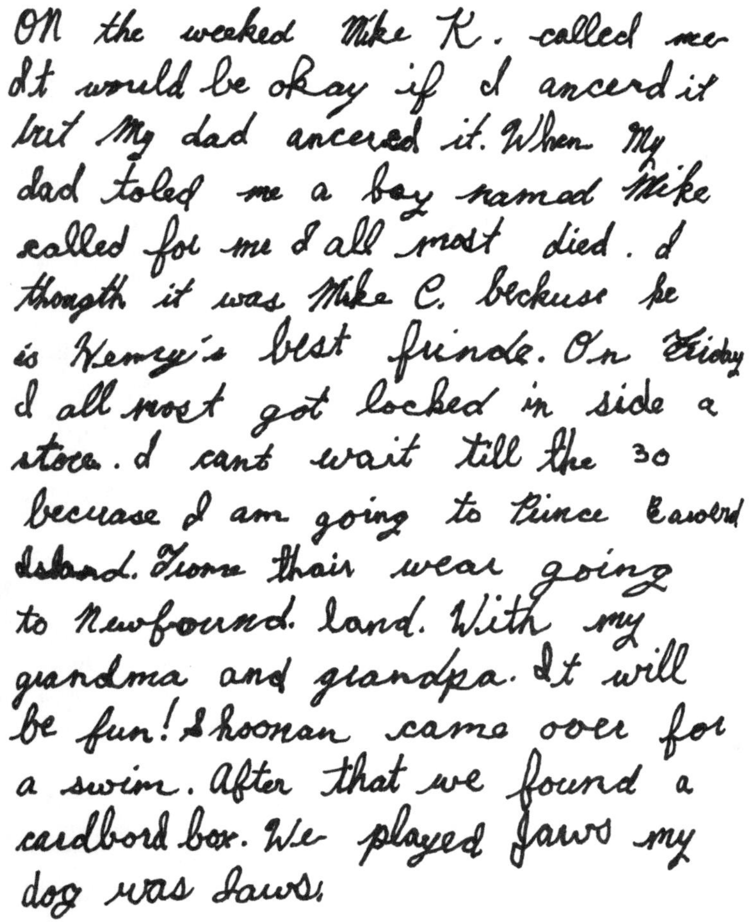
On the weeked Mike K. called me
It would be okay if I ancerd it
but My dad ancered it. When My
dad toled me a boy namad Mike
called for me I all most died. I
thougth it was Mike C. beckuse he
is Henry's best frinde. On Friday
I all most got locked in side a
store. I cant wait till the 30
becuase I am going to Prince Edward
Island. From thair wear going
to Newfound. land. With my
grandma and grandpa. It will
be fun! Shoonan came over for
a swim. After that we found a
cardbord box. We played Jaws my
dog was Jaws.

FIGURE 3.7 *INDEPENDENT SPELLER*

can we make about this student's spelling? One noticeable feature is her use of compound words almost (all most), inside (in side). Her functional spellings are examples of **transpositional** spelling strategies: on thought (thougth), friend (frinde), because (becuase). It is interesting to track the spelling of the word "because." She made two attempts: "beckuse" and then "becuase."

In the first attempt, she combines the "c" and "k," which both represent the same sound; and a few lines later we see a transpositional spelling, with all the letters present but in the wrong order. Why does this happen? One hypothesis might be that on the first attempt she uses the phonological or sound system and on the second attempt she uses a visual system. Within a short span, this student knew that the first attempt (beckuse) did not look like the conventional form, so she abandoned her sound system and searched for a form of the word that "looked" right.

ESL Students and Spelling

Students learning English as a second language need experiences that will combine all of the communication systems. Initially, ESL students need to be read to and have conversations about stories. Many of the stories may be about personal experiences. Through talk they formulate pictures about events. Drawing a picture is easier than writing for the ESL student because it does not require them to think in their native language and then translate into English. Drawing and illustrating facilitates putting thoughts down on paper and should be followed by talking about the pictures. Sentences can be transcribed at the bottom of the drawings and read aloud. ESL students need time to establish a data bank of English language words.

Because language is socially driven, it is important for ESL students to have experiences that allow them to talk, share, and ask questions. They need to see and hear language being used. Strategies teachers might use to help ESL students develop and write a story would be to put sentences on strips of paper and then invite students to fit the pieces of the story together. Such strategies extend their knowledge about syntax, semantics, and graphophonemics. Children need to make sense out of language by establishing meaning, and language learning is learning how to mean (Halliday, 1977). Making sense out of language is at the forefront of the language development for ESL students. As they make sense out of the English language, they use it more often, extending and refining their use of cueing systems.

Students with Learning Disabilities and Spelling

Some, but not all, students with LD are reluctant to write and spell, for many reasons. Depending on the nature of the learning disability, it may be appropriate to allow them to use a computer to write. Many students with LD are identified as visual, tactile, and kinesthetic. These perceptual preferences lend themselves to computer use: tapping keys on a keyboard is tactile, sitting in a computer chair which swivels or rocks is kinesthetic, and viewing results on the screen is visual.

Another issue involving students with LD concerns cursive writing. Many students with LD prefer printing because cursive writing requires a considerable amount of energy and concentration. This may be seen by watching how students with LD grasp a pencil. They squeeze it hard and press firmly, often breaking the lead. It does not take long for them to tire, become frustrated, and give up. Printing or using a computer can help reduce the amount of energy these students have to use.

Surface-Level Scores (SLS)

When doing assessments, writing teachers should complete a "surface-level score" (SLS). This score represents an overall percentage of the conventional-to-functional spellings. In Figure 3.3, this piece contained a total of 42 words with 13 words (31 percent) functional, and 29 (69 percent) words spelled conventionally. When monitoring a student's development over time, patterns may emerge in surface-level scores across different writing genres. For instance, a personal journal may exhibit an SLS consistently at a 85 to 90 percent accuracy range. A low SLS (60 to 65 percent) may be related to the complexity of vocabulary the student used. A drop in accuracy level may reveal that the student attempted to use more complex language. Students in upper grades (grades 4 to 8) can be taught to monitor their own SLS. This information can be used when reporting to parents to show them what to look for in their child's writing. It can help parents who become concerned when they find spelling errors in their child's writing.

Summary

When working on spelling and writing with students, it is important to identify the characteristics of reluctant, developing, and independent spellers. Interest and context are often the key to learning style, but students should not be judged as being only one type of speller. For instance, a child who likes to write about his or her favorite music groups or fashions may exhibit characteristics of an independent writer. At other times, when the child is expected to write outside of the "comfort levels," he or she may exhibit characteristics of a developing writer. A child's development as a speller and writer can be tracked by using writing folders or portfolios to maintain an ongoing record. Tracking writing is covered in more depth in Chapter 4.

TEACHER STORY • *Letter Writing*

Simone L. Ecola
Grade 6, University Public School
Detroit, Michigan

I am a sixth-grade teacher who has struggled with the writing process. Since the beginning of the school year I worked with Gerry Oglan on developing my writing program. I taught a lesson on friendly letter-writing and incorporated the "I wishes" that Gerry had demonstrated for the staff. I liked how the wishes helped students to focus on revising their text. I had planned a trip to New York prior to September 11. Because of the events of that day, I seized the opportunity to get my students involved in letter writing. My plan was to hand deliver the letters to New York City firefighters. Initially, students were hesitant, but by using wishes, along with reading and discussing their stories with others in the class, they soon felt comfortable sharing their work with at least three other people in the class. Students worked from a draft, incorporating information from others. When they felt their letter was done, they did conventional editing for grammar and punctuation. All of the students felt good writing for a real audience. Figure 3.8 shows the letter Ashley wrote to the New York firefighters.

Dear Firefighters of New York City,   11-14-01

I'm very appreciative of all the lives you saved. I am very happy to know that when a life needs to be saved you'll be there. When a house is on fire I am glad to know you'll be there, also we can definitely depend on you.

    I appreciate all the work and love you put into being so helpful you believe in the most important thing and that's love for all people.

    I hope you keep doing what you do best and that's saving lives.

               Sincerely yours,

               Ashley Harris
               Ashley Harris

4

Writing for Publication

Many teachers operate under the assumption that writing should involve a series of stages commonly identified as prewriting, writing, revising, and publication. Progressing through the stages should produce a polished text that has been revised and edited by students. However, a common concern expressed by teachers revolves around the issue of revision and editing. As an example, one teacher stated that in her writing program she lets her students write about subjects they are interested in. When they are done, she holds conferences with them about their stories, and then she revises their stories and gives them back, asking the students to copy them over with the revisions. This closed model approach is problematic because it removes the student author from the two most important steps in the process: revision and editing. To have an effective and dynamic writing program, teachers should support an open model, especially as it applies to revision and editing.

In a closed model, the writing process is controlled not by the writer but from the outside—by other people and by structures that must be followed in an orderly fashion. As a result, ownership of writing (and text) rests outside of the author, and the focus is on producing a product to be evaluated by others. These conditions rarely result in powerful writing, but teachers are more concerned with whether the student has met a preconceived set of requirements.

In contrast, in an open model writing is controlled by students. They are encouraged to write in a variety of genres (e.g., letters to pen pals, postcards, invitations, biographies, and so on) as a means of exploring different language patterns. By giving students ownership of the writing process, they can focus on meaning (semantics), a key part of the process that allows students to be self-reflective and therefore more engaged in what they are doing. Ownership is highly recursive—students continually revisit their text and produce drafts and rewrite because *they* are not satisfied with content. Students drive the revision and editing process because they, not the teacher, own the text.

Writing for publication involves a process of revision and editing. During revision and editing students are required to make changes to their texts through two processes: The first, revision, involves clarifying the text for meaning. The second, editing, deals with the surface-level features of the text and requires students to edit for accuracy or conventions (spelling, punctuation, and grammar). In doing both revision and editing, students learn about graphophonemics (sound/letter relationships), syntax (grammar and word order), semantics (prior knowledge), and pragmatics (language and social settings). The following outlines how teachers can implement revision and editing in their writing programs and how they can shift the responsibility for the writing from a closed model to an open model. Taking time at the start of the year to establish the framework for revision and editing places teachers in a position to act as members of the writing community, facilitators in every sense of the word, not directing and marking but guiding and questioning. Implementation may take approximately three weeks, depending on the students and the comfort level of the teacher. It is important for teachers to take ample time to ensure that students understand their role and that of the teachers' in the writing process.

Week One: Revision

Revision focuses on the identification of unclear or confusing text. During the first week, the teacher selects a different text to show the class each day. The selected texts can be stories developed by the teacher that reflect the age and writing patterns of their students, or text from student journals. (Permission should be granted by the student.) The teacher reads the text to the class and invites students to think of "wishes" they would offer to the author of the text. Young writers think, talk, and write in generalizations. These generalizations include the use of common nouns and vague statements that are void of detail and do not inform the reader. Revision should provide the necessary detail to enrich the writing and help the text flow. The writing samples given in this chapter can be used as examples of how text moves through revision first and then through conventional editing. The following is a sample of a story written by a fourth-grade student.

I went to my aunts cottage with my cousins.
We had tokens by doing things. I came in second.
I won five dollars and fifty cents, stickers and a
t-shirt. First place got a t-shirt and a candle.

In this piece we see generalizations in the text. They include the use of common nouns (aunt, cousins), as well as vague information about winning tokens, money, t-shirts, and a candle. To help the student revise this text, the teacher introduces the concept of "listening editors." The role of these student editors is to listen to a student author read their text, and then offer feedback. The feedback comes in the form of "wishes"—positive feedback techniques that avoid negative or sarcastic remarks. Wishes or questions posed by listening editors demonstrate that a writer cannot assume what a reader knows. In response to the story shown earlier, the listening editors offered the following wishes to the author:

I wish you would have said where your aunt's
    cottage was located.
I wish you would have described what was involved
    in winning tokens.
I wish you would have written the names of your
    aunt and cousins.

Once listening editors provide the author with their wishes it is then up to the author to incorporate some or all of the wishes. After decisions are made about what to incorporate into the text, the author may request another session with the listening editors for more feedback. Lucy Calkins (1991) considers questioning to be an act of revision. She believes reflecting on our thoughts or those of others and asking questions underlies not only revision but thought itself. Revision must precede conventional editing. Why? Because revision allows students to think about meaning before focusing on conventional editing and grammatical structures. Nancy Atwell (1987) believes the focus of revision should not be on conventional editing because it detracts from revision by making accuracy and perfection the focus. Revision should change and alter text so that what is published is different from the original idea or draft.

Teachers and students who focus on editorial issues in early drafts are de-emphasizing information and disallowing the real possibility that revision will allow for changes of such magnitude that the final draft will be significantly different. (Atwell, 1987, p. 106)

Over the course of the week the teacher may notice students dropping the "I wish" part and moving to questions such as, "What is the aunt's name?" or "Where was the aunt's cottage?" Teachers should not be overly concerned when the shift to direct questioning occurs. At this point, teachers invite pairs or groups of students to rewrite the text incorporating the wishes, as shown here.

My Weekend

I went to my Aunt Lisa's cottage near Los Angeles, California. I played with my cousins, Louisa and Scott and we watched the movie Mr. Holland's Opus and played board games, Monopoly, Sorry and Trouble.

When I got home in San Diego California, I went outside and played Tag with my friends.

My mom and dad took me to Target and bought me some jeans and sweat shirts for school.

My birthday is coming soon. It is on Sept. 17. I'm going to invite all my friends.

The difference in the revised piece is dramatic. By incorporating the wishes from her peers this student provided more information and detail for the reader. In this case, the teacher asked the student to read the revised text to the class and invited the class to generate new wishes based on the revised story. The class made the following suggestions:

Do you like your aunt?

What is Target?

What kind of tag did you play?

Why did you go to Target if it is a store?

Do you like your friends?

What part of San Diego do you live in?

How did you get home?
Did you find the trip fast or slow?

It is interesting to note that in the second round of wishes the students dropped the "I wish" part and went straight to asking questions.

From the first set of three wishes proposed by the class, to the second set of eight wishes, it is clear the class took a more sophisticated semantic stance toward the text. Their questions relate to more detail about aspects of the story and subsequently were considering their audience or reader. At this point the student rewrote their story.

I went to my favorite Aunt Lisa's cottage near Los Angles California. I played with my cousins Louisa and Scott and we watched the movie Mr. Holland's Opus and played board games, Monopoly, Sorry and Trouble.

When I got home in San Diego California I went outside and played frozen tag with my best friends, Lauren, Katie and Jackie.

My mom and dad took me to a store named Target and bought me some jeans and sweatshirts.

My birthday is coming soon. It's on Sept. 17. I'm going to have a birthday party and I'm going to invite all my friends. I can't wait!

It is important to point out that the author decided to use some of the suggestions but not all of them. For instance, she responded to the first question (Do you like your aunt?) by adding the adjective "favorite" to describe her feelings for her aunt. In answer to the third question (What kind of tag did you play?) she described it as "frozen tag" and added the names of her friends. But she also chose not to answer the questions about what part of San Diego she lives in, or how she got home. At this point, the author was satisfied with the revisions and decided to stop revising her writing. Throughout the revision process, students were always in control of the text.

Week Two: Conventional Editing

Conventional editing takes place following revision and deals with spelling, punctuation, and grammar. Using the same group of stories written in the first week, the teacher rewrites the stories inserting invented spellings, and grammar and punctuation error patterns:

```
On the weekend I went camping with my
scot pak. we left on friday and and
returnd on sunday afternoon. While we
there we had to set up our won tents
we had diferent jobs to do. There
wer for of is in my tent and and it was
hard to sleep because evryone was
talking. The scot leders taught us some
new games. We also did sirvivel
activities and they wer a lot of fun.
before we left the camp on Sunday we had
to take doen our tents, clean up the
camp and load up for a long rid home
Most of us were very tird by the time we
got home. I spent the rest if Sunday
watching televison.
```

The teacher then introduces editing codes:

Spelling ∪∪∪		Insert a Word ∧
Punctuation ◯		Remove a Word ( )
Grammar ▭		
Capital ▢		

Students once again work in pairs, using the editing codes to mark the error patterns in the text:

```
On the weekend I went camping with my

scot pak. we left on friday and (and)

returnd on sunday afternoon. While we

there we had to set up our won tents

we had diferent jobs to do. There

wer for of is in my tent and and it was

hard to sleep because evryone was

talking. The scot leders taught us some

new games. We also did sirvivel

activities and they wer a lot of fun.

before we left the camp on Sunday we had

to take doen our tents, clean up the

camp and load up for a long rid home

Most of us were very tird by the time we

got home. I spent the rest if Sunday

watching televison.
```

Once the students have edited the text, a copy of the story is placed on the overhead or on chart paper. Reading through each sentence, the teacher invites students to identify and explain where they think a certain editing code should appear in the story and why. When students feel they have highlighted all of the error patterns, the teacher confirms the codes and adds any the students may have missed. Teachers should note that when students start to edit text during writer's workshop (discussed later in this chapter), they will come across grammatical structures not listed on the editing codes. For instance, they may come across the need for quotation marks or a new paragraph. When this occurs the teacher should introduce the problem to the class, conduct a minilesson on the grammatical structure in question, develop a code, and add it to the coding chart. Students then learn new grammatical structures in context.

During conventional editing, students use many of the communication and cueing systems: reading, writing, speaking, listening, viewing, and representing, along with syntax, and graphophonemics. Once again, it is important for the teacher to allow time for students to experience conventional editing through this process.

Week Three: Pulling It Together

During this week, students are provided with a text in need of revision and conventional editing. They work in pairs or small groups, first on revision, then on conventional editing. This is a good time for teachers to vary composition of the groups because students have a tendency to work with their friends, often ignoring others. There is not a set procedure for deciding who will work with whom. Some teachers assign pairs, grouping reluctant and developing writers with independent writers; whereas others start from a social perspective, allowing students to choose partners, with the understanding that, over the course of the year, they must work with everyone in the class.

From the start, it is important to emphasize the teacher's role during writing for publication. Teachers evaluate students based on who they revise and edit with and how well they work together. In so doing, teachers help developing and evolving writers by providing them with opportunities to work with independent writers, who can model and demonstrate semantic revision and conventional editing.

Writing for Publication: Writer's Workshop

Writing for publication is part of a writer's workshop approach. While students are expected to write and publish pieces of their own work, they also take turns acting as listening and conventional editors. Writer's workshop usually takes place twice a week, allowing anywhere from 45 to 60 minutes or more each time. Large blocks of time are preferred because it allows students the time they need for revision and editing. Teachers using a thematic approach in their classrooms may allocate more time to writer's workshop. Once teachers complete the three weeks of practice with revision and editing, they introduce writer's workshop. Students should be provided with folders for their drafts. Also, there should be an area in the room designated as an "editor's table." The editor's table should be equipped with:

- Dictionaries
- Thesauri
- Pencils
- Erasers
- Tray for rough drafts marked "To Be Edited"
- Tray for edited drafts marked "Edited"
- Tray for drafts marked "To Be Published"
- Scrap paper
- Editing codes

Selecting Editors

Teachers have found that it works best to assign students to be conventional editors. This allows them to group reluctant writers with more confident or experienced writers, or allow independent writers to work together. Students are assigned as conventional editors for a one-week period. This allows time for talking and sharing ideas, and gives everyone in the class a turn at editing during the school year. During writer's workshop, conventional editors are not allowed to work on their own writing. Why? Student editors who are also working on their own stories often rush through conventional editing of another student's text because they want to return to their own writing. This leads to partially edited text with a great deal of error patterns. There is usually plenty of work in need of editing during writer's workshop; however, if there are moments when there is no work to be edited, then conventional editors can help other students with their writing.

Usually four or five students are selected each week to act as conventional editors. A large number of editors is needed to cover a range of skill levels. According to Vygotsky's (1978) "zone of proximal development," students who may not possess skills in revision and editing themselves benefit from speaking and listening to students who do. At times teachers may need to hold a conference with a group of students during writer's workshop to assist them with revision and editing. This is a good time to conduct minilessons on a variety of topics related to writing. Some teachers like to provide editors with plastic visors or hats or let the students bring in baseball hats. Students like this because it adds drama to the role.

Listening editors are allowed to work on their own writing, while occasionally taking the time to listen to a student who may need feedback on a story. Teachers may vary the listening editors. Generally, each story is read to two listening editors, and the listening editors initial the draft so that the teacher can see that the author fulfilled this requirement.

Writer's Workshop in Action

Prior to implementing writer's workshop the following should be in place:

- Three weeks of revision and editing
- The editor's table
- A review of classroom rules and routines

To make writer's workshop a success, classroom rules and routines must be well-understood by all students. Everyone must know their roles and how the classroom operates during the writer's workshop.

Listening Editors

During writer's workshop, students in need of listening editors ask one or two of the assigned listening editors to listen while they read their stories. This can take place on the floor, in the hallway, or at a designated place in the classroom. Listening editors listen to the story, offer wishes, and initial the draft. The author is required to consider and select or add new information to incorporate into his or her stories.

Assigning listening editors varies from teacher to teacher. Some teachers like to assign six students each week as listening editors, which gives everyone in the class an opportunity to listen to stories and offer feedback at some point in the year. Others teachers feel comfortable letting students select whomever they like to be their listening editors. This approach raises a social issue: Students have a tendency to ask their friends to listen to their stories, often resulting in students talking about issues other than revision. In the writer's workshop approach, the teacher, who knows the class, is in a better position to make these assignments.

When students feel that the meaning and the message they want to convey has been accomplished, the story is placed in a tray located at the editor's table called "To Be Edited." The author is then free to work on another piece.

Conventional Editors

Three trays are placed at the editor's table: one marked "To Be Edited," another marked "Edited," and the third marked "To Be Published." When authors are done with the revision and are satisfied with the content of the story, they place their piece in the "To Be Edited" tray. Conventional editors take drafts from the "To Be Edited" tray, and, working in pairs, mark the error patterns, using the coding system established by the class. If the conventional editors come across something in the text they are not sure of they may ask the author for clarification.

Once the piece has been edited using the codes, the piece is placed in the "Edited" tray. When writer's workshop starts, students are expected to check the "Edited" tray to see if any of their text has been edited. It is their responsibility to take the text and begin to make the surface-level changes (punctuation, spelling, grammar, etc.). Authors may ask the editors for clarification or may even request a conference with the teacher. Once a student has finished the conventional editing, he or she places the piece in the "To Be Published" tray. This tray is reserved for the teacher, who examines the piece for the quality of revision and editing. If the teacher notices information that editors missed, such as spelling, punctuation, or grammar, it can be sent back to the conventional editors, and a conference with the student author may be needed. The "To Be Published" tray acts as a "check and balance" for the teacher. The teacher wants to ensure that conventional editors are doing their jobs and that listening editors are providing feedback during listening or revision. During writer's workshop, teachers should be free to circulate around the classroom, holding conferences, observing, and making suggestions, but not leading the class. This is a good time for teachers to record anecdotal notes, for assessment purposes, on each student.

Tracking Writing

With so many people doing so many different things during writer's workshop a tracking system is needed. By using a tracking system teachers are aware what students are working on and where they are in the publication process. Atwell (1987) uses a strategy he calls "Status of the Class." Building on the same process, a "Teacher Observation and Tracking Sheet" is suggested (see Figure 4.1).

An important part of a successful writing program involves knowing what students are working on. This does two things: First, it allows teachers to track student progress. Second, it sends a strong message to students that they are being monitored and that ownership and accountability rests with them. Writing workshop begins by recording every student's name on the tracking sheet. Before students start writing, each person is asked to state what they are working on and the status of the writing. This information is recorded in the box and coded. The next day, the process is repeated, and over time, patterns emerge from the class. For instance, some students may be spending too much time on a certain text, signaling a need for a writing conference. Other students may be moving too

Status Codes: **Draft — D**
Editing — E
Publishing — P

Name	Date	Date	Date
	Story: _____ Status: _____	Story: _____ Status: _____	Story: _____ Status: _____
	Story: _____ Status: _____	Story: _____ Status: _____	Story: _____ Status: _____
	Story: _____ Status: _____	Story: _____ Status: _____	Story: _____ Status: _____

FIGURE 4.1   *TEACHER OBSERVATION AND TRACKING SHEET*

quickly, not taking enough time for semantic revision. Writing for publication requires a deadline. By using the tracking sheet, teachers will be in a better position to help students anytime during the process and help them to meet deadlines.

Revision with Young Children

Revision begins in kindergarten and Grade 1. It may not look like the kind of revision that occurs in upper grades, but communication and cueing systems still apply. Young children use viewing and representing almost exclusively: They build things out of sand, use Legos, make cities and towers from large and small wooden blocks, dress up, and role play. But they also use speaking to share their creations with the teacher and the class. When teachers read a story to young children and talk about the content, they encourage speaking and listening (and viewing if it is a picture book). Children who are asked to draw or illustrate part of a story that meant a lot to them should be given time to share the picture with another student. Using a strategy like "Three Pluses and a Wish" allows teachers to initiate semantic revision: Students say three things they like about a drawing and one thing they wish the author had included in the picture. (Young students may want to start with one "plus" and one "wish.") For example, a first-grade student sharing a drawing drew the following plus and wish from another student: "I really liked the way you drew the dog. I wish you would have put in a picture of the sun." The author of the picture then went and drew in the sun. This is an example of how sharing can provide positive feedback. Will it happen all of the time? Maybe not, but the key point is to have students share their work and let others offer comments. When first-graders start writing, they can do the same with their written work. Sharing with others demonstrates to young writers that talking is a part of authoring. Students progress through school writing not as a closed but an open and interpretive process.

Summary

Writing for publication requires students to use two key elements. The first is revision, which is the focus of writing and publishing. Revision requires students to revisit their writing and, with the help of others, make changes to the text, which will make it more enjoyable for the audience who will be reading the text. Second is editing, which should always follow revisions and should not take place until the author is satisfied with the content of the text. Listening and speaking act as the impetus for revisions and editing to take place. Through conversations, students negotiate their text, moving it to deeper levels of meaning.

The next chapter looks at a genre approach to writing. Once revision, editing, routines, and expectations are established, a genre approach provides a format for the writer's workshop and a range of writing experiences that encourage communication and cueing systems.

TEACHER STORY • *Writing about Art*

Anita Ricks-Bates
Fine Arts Teacher, Grade 8
University Public School
Detroit, Michigan

My goal was to have students be able to write about art in a descriptive manner; so I introduced them to the idea of wishes. Many times when students are asked to look at a work of art and assess it they will say either, "Oh, I like it" or "I don't like it." They are often too vague in their descriptions. To begin the thinking process, we started with a discussion of art in terms of the five elements: line, shape, color, value, and texture. The children were then asked to make a list of the three primary colors and the three secondary colors.

RED	YELLOW	BLUE
ORANGE	GREEN	PURPLE

Underneath each color they were instructed to make a list of things that they perceived to be associated with that particular color.

Kourtney's Word List

RED	YELLOW	BLUE
blood	peppers	blueberries
ketchup	lemon	sky
apple	butter	water
peppers	cheese	blue jeans
strawberries	bannanas	saphire
cherries	squash	blue jays
tomatoes	sun	
ruby	mustard	
raspberries	Tweety	
fruit punch		
crimson		

ORANGE	GREEN	PURPLE
orange	apples	grapes
necterine	grass	plum
cheese	trees	lilac
leaves	chives	
	lettuce	
	alligator	
	pickle	
	guacomole	
	peridot birthstone	
	emerald	
	Statue of Liberty	
	jungle	

In another word list exercise, the students listed emotions that they associated with a particular color. Once the lists of emotions were made, we went back and discussed adjectives that could be substituted for words that they already knew. For example, underneath the color blue, the word "sad" was mostly used. "Sad" was then substituted by the word "melancholy".

After our word list session, the idea of a wish list was initiated with the following text:

```
This picture has a lot of colors. It has
some shapes and some colors in it. There is
also some writing on it. It is a picture of
somebody's artwork. I feel things when I
look at it.
```

The children were separated into four groups and given a piece of artwork to look at. I asked them to read the text in relationship to the artwork (a reproduction of a self-portrait by Vincent van Gogh). I then introduced the concept of making a wish. Some of the children were baffled by this, so I gave them an example: If I were reading this text and looking at this painting, I might say that I wish the writer had told me more about color, specifically, types of colors. The children were instructed that they were allowed to work with one another for feedback. The following is Kourtney's wish list:

Wish List - I Wish the Writer Would Have . . .

1) Said what kind of colors there were

2) Listed the shapes and colors in the painting

3) Quoted the writing in the picture

4) Told who has done the painting

5) Explained how he felt about this picture

Students were then asked to revise the story incorporating their wishes and use any words from their word list. The following is Kourtney's revision from the original text.

Art, 2nd Hour
September 4, 2001

In the painting I am viewing, looks like a European man in his middle ages. This man stands big and tall and behing him looks like a whole multitude of people made of dots. This man is Vincent Van Gogh. These dots to represent people are a flesh-colored red that looks like faces to to me. Also in this crowd of people, there is baby blue, midnight blue, and a grass-colored green to represent their clothing. As well, the green can represent landscaping. The little bit of black can be the small space between these people. There is also jungle green in this painting that also represent grass and plants. Van Gogh, the man in this picture, has an oval shaped head and high cheek bones, medium-sized ear, with a receeding headline. His hair is mixed with light, vibrant colors such as butter yellow, tangerine orange, guacomole green, a small amount of black, and crimson. All of these colors all come together as blonde. His flesh on his forehead is very bright because of the light, but the rest of his skin in yellow, red, and peachy orange. The right side of his forehead his jungle green. His eyebrows are is the color of a pickel.

5

Word Study

Word study deals with sounds, letters, and their relationships, and is integral to the graphophonemic cueing system. It is one of the most common strategies used by teachers and usually involves word games, such as crossword puzzles, word searchers, Scrabble, and many computer games and programs. The purpose of word study is to provide students with experiences that explore relationships between the written graphemes (one or more letters working as a unit) and the phonemes (a single sound that distinguishes one word from another) they represent. At times, word study may take the form of word analysis; for example, when students are asked to look at patterns in roots, prefixes, and suffixes, or to find as many words as they can from a large word, such as "encyclopedia." At other times, word study may take the form of a vocabulary lesson. Teachers who use thematic units as their instructional approach may focus on word families. For instance, a teacher working on a winter theme may spend time having his or her students explore words that relate to winter. The term "word study" refers to many aspects of words—their sound/letter relationships, their origins, and patterns within words. The focus is not necessarily on the rules that govern the English language and spelling but rather on the exploration and discovery of patterns, along with sound/letter relationships. Word study and spelling build students' knowledge about words so they will be able to write using more complex language.

Word Study, Patterns, Rules, and the Brain

Spelling Rules

The English language is made up of 26 letters (5 vowels and 21 consonants). The traditional way for learning new letters and sounds supported a closed model. Words were divided into their individual letters, and students were taught rules associated with the letters, which they were expected to memorize and apply to words they wanted to write or spell. There are two problems associated with this approach: The first has to do with the large number of rules that govern the use of vowels and consonants. There are so many that it is difficult for students to remember and apply all of them. However, rules can be useful when students develop their own. For instance, one fifth-grade teacher had his students complete a word-hunt strategy (see Figure 5.3). Students located words from their personal journals that they had difficulty spelling and wrote them in the first column. (Some students have difficulty finding misspelled words in their own writing. It may be necessary for someone to help them or to pair them with a more capable speller.) They were then asked to try spelling the word again in the second column. Then, the teacher wrote the conventional spelling in the third column and invited the students to think of a rule they could apply to the spelling of this word or a similar word. Some examples of rules that students developed are:

> Rule for the word "muscle." Pretend the "c" is a flexing muscle.
> Rule for the word "Scottish." Two "t's" because they drink a lot of tea.
> Rule for the word "chocolate." "C" and "s" have the same sound. For the word chocolate I think of the word "cocoa."

When students develop rules that support their knowledge of the English language, rules are more meaningful. The second problem relates to what neuroscience is suggesting about the brain and learning to spell.

The Brain and Spelling

Brain scientists suggest that good spellers have strong visual memories: They remember words more by the way they look than by the way they sound. Scientists also suggest that the brain "chunks" information by forming it into patterns that the brain internalizes. Once a word has been internalized it will not be forgotten. Bill Bryson (1990), in his book, *The*

Mother Tongue: English and How It Got That Way, illustrates the notion of visual memory and spelling using the following:

> ***Just a quick test to see if you can tell which of the following are mispelled:***

supercede	irresistable
conceed	rhythym
procede	opthalmologist
idiosyncracy	diptheria
concensus	anamoly
accomodate	afficianado
dexterious	caesarian
impressario	grafitti

Most people will find it difficult to identify how many words are misspelled (including the one in the sentence that introduces the list). Brain scientists would say the problem is not with reading the words but with internalizing the correct spellings. Why? Most people initially rely on sounding the word out rather than on visually memorizing it. Whenever parents or teachers try this activity the first thing they want to do is write the words they are not sure of. Many of them write three or four versions of a word like "accommodate":

acommodate
accomodate
acomodate
accommodate

When they finish writing their list it helps them to see which of the four options is correct, moving from relying on sound to using visual memory. Memorized words do not stay in our long-term memories, but words we internalize will. Why? Part of it has to do with "frequency of use." If you worked for an ophthalmologist and you used the word "ophthalmologist" on a regular basis, then spelling it would not be an issue. Personal interest and emotion also help with internalization. If you are a woman and you had to have a cesarean section during the birth of a child, the experience and emotional attachment would be strong enough for you to remember the spelling. The same effect can be applied to first- and second-graders. First- and second-grade teachers wonder why students can spell words such as "tyrannosaurus" and yet have trouble with simple words such as "said." The emotional attachment kids have to dinosaurs and the pleasure they experience from looking at pictures and words about them facilitates internalization of the spellings. The more separated information and skills are from prior knowledge and actual experience the more dependence there is on rote memory and repetition (Caine & Caine, 1991). Robert Sylwester (1995) states, "We know emotion is very important to the educative process because it drives attention, which drives learning and memory" (p. 72).

There are only around 400 irregular spellings in the English language, of which 84 percent conform to a general pattern (e.g. purse/nurse/curse, patch/catch/latch) while only 3 percent of our words are spelled in a really unpredictable way. Back to Bryson's (1990) spelling list:

All of the words are spelled wrong, and the correct spellings are:

supersede/supercede	irresistible
concede	rhythm
proceed	ophthalmologist
idiosyncrasy	diphtheria
consensus	anomaly
accommodate	aficionado/afficionado
dexterous/dextrous	cesarean/cesarian
impresario	graffiti

Classroom Strategies

Word Webs

Using patterns to teach about words involves a range of strategies. Rhyming patterns are the most common, but word webs work very well. Students, working in pairs or small groups, are given a word such as "ant" and are asked to find and write as many words as they can that contain the word (see Figure 5.1).

Encourage students to use any book (science, social studies, mathematics) in the class to look for the words. There are two rules to remember when using word webs: First, students using a text, or even a dictionary, think the more words they have the better the web. So, be sure to tell them they have to know the meaning of any word they place on the word web. If they cannot give the meaning then they will have to remove it from the web. The second rule involves the correct spelling of the words. Any word on the web must be spelled correctly. This will prevent students from guessing at the spelling for the sake of placing words on the web.

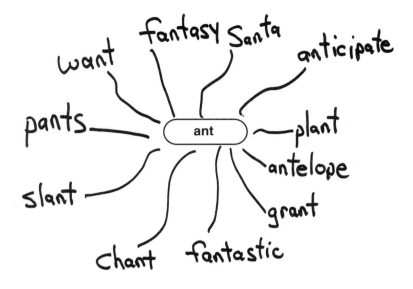

FIGURE 5.1 *A WORD WEB*

Word Hunts

Word hunts involve using personal journals. Students are invited to go back through their personal journals and find words they think are misspelled. They write the word on a "word hunt sheet" (see Figure 5.2)

In this example, Jarrod listed the misspelled words he found in the "Invented Spellings" column. In the "One More Try" column he tried spelling the word again, making changes he thought would make the word conventional. When he got to the "Actual Spelling" column, Jarrod was able to ask someone about the accuracy of his first two attempts, look the word up in the dictionary or thesaurus, and then sit with the teacher and have a conference about the words. Here is a good place to encourage students to develop their own rules to remember the spelling of words. Jarrod stated that "c" and "s" have the same sound, indicating his knowledge about these sounds and how he uses his own rules to remember how to spell "chocolate." The spelling is framed and internalized in something that has personal and emotional meaning. Remembering this rule will be much easier for Jarrod than would a general spelling rule. Emotion maximizes the memory system and facilitates cognition.

Word Hunt

Name: Jarrod

Date:

Title: Word Hunt

INVENTED SPELLING	ONE MORE TRY!	ACTUAL SPELLING
reciaver	reciver	receiver
pices	pises	pieces
Chocelate	chocolate	chocolate
yesturday	yesterday	yesterday

COMMENTS: (Can you find a pattern or think of a rule that might help you to remember how to spell these words?)

The C and S have the same sound. For the word chocolate think of the word coco. (I spelled it choc⊗ate) I just took the h off, c(h)oco.

FIGURE 5.2 *WORD HUNT SHEET*

Word Grids

Word grids are by far one of the most popular word study strategies. Students are given a grid (see Figure 5.3) and are asked to place an "X" in the top left-hand corner. As this is a four-letter word grid, they must write a word that contains four letters across the top of the grid, placing one letter in each square, and going down the left side of the grid.

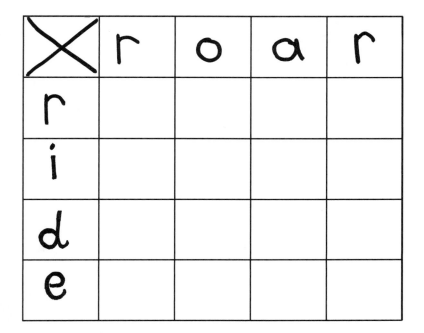

FIGURE 5.3   *WORD GRID*

Using the words "roar" and "ride" as an example, students would then be asked to write a word in the first column that begins with an "r" and ends with an "r." They may use any text in the room to find words or may choose words from the word wall, chart stories, and so on. In the next square they are asked to find a word that begins with an "r" and ends with an "o." Continuing to the next square they look for a word that starts with "r" and ends with "a," and finally a word that begins with an "r" and ends with an "r" (see Figure 5.4). Students must fill in all the squares on the grid.

Some things to consider when using word grids: Students should use only words they know the meanings of, and the words must be spelled correctly. The fact that it is a four-letter word grid does not mean the only words students can use in the squares are four-letter words. In Figure 5.4, a three-letter word ("rio") was used in one square and a six-letter word ("Russia") in another. The purpose of word grids is to let students explore words, regardless of their length. A variation on this strategy can include using the same four-letter word across the top and along the left side. Either way the process remains the same.

Another approach would be to use theme words. Some teachers have created a large word grid on a bulletin board and invited students to add

	r	o	a	r
r	rear	rio	Russia	river
i				
d				
e				

FIGURE 5.4   *WORD GRID*

words to the grid throughout the week or month. Students working on a large grid in pairs or small groups experience success because they are collaborating and negotiating the words that will go on the grid. In essence, they are using language to learn about language. This kind of socialization allows students to use one another as resources. Teachers find that conversation around sounds, letters, and their relationships increases substantially, which confirms research that talk acts as a "conduit" between thinking and speech (Vygotsky, 1978).

Personal Spelling List

Teachers and parents always ask about weekly spelling tests. The personal spelling list is an alternative to a weekly list. Students can select words from a theme or a subject, or they may select words from an area of interest, such as sports (see Figure 5.5).

During the week students spend time studying their words in class and at home. On Friday they pair up and exchange their lists. Each person dictates their spelling list to someone else using the "Personal Dictation Sheet." Students then mark each other's sheet, sign the bottom, and turn

Personal Spelling List

Name: _____

Week of: _____

_____   _____
_____   _____
_____   _____
_____   _____
_____   _____
_____   _____
_____   _____
_____   _____
_____   _____
_____   _____
_____   _____

FIGURE 5.5   *PERSONAL SPELLING LIST*

it in to the teacher, who checks the list and signs it. At this point, the sheets can be sent home for parents to sign and write a comment at the bottom of the page. Students may also want to write a comment related to their spelling for the week (see Figure 5.6).

Other strategies teachers can use may include some of the following:

Proprietary words–Company or trade names (e.g., Burger King, K-Mart, Radio Shack)

Acronyms–Words that are formed by joining the first letters of other words, such as NATO (North Atlantic Treaty Organization), MASH (Mobile Army Surgical Hospital).

Personal Dictation Sheet

Name: _____ Date: _____

Subject: _____

_____	_____
_____	_____
_____	_____
_____	_____
_____	_____
_____	_____
_____	_____
_____	_____

Dictated by: _____

Checked by: _____

Comments: _____

_____

_____

FIGURE 5.6 *PERSONAL DICTATION SHEET*

Anagrams–Words or phrases that contain the same letters but are in a different order (e.g., agree/eager, ocean/canoe).

Palindromes–Word, phrase, verse, or sentence that reads the same backward and forward (e.g., deed, radar).

Abbreviations–Letters that represent words (e.g., Mr./Mister, MI/Michigan).

Commercial Games

There are a number of commercial games and word puzzles available at department stores that are suitable for the development of word study.

Scrabble, Spill and Spell, Word Searchers, and Crosswords allow students to study language outside of the writing program.

Technology

Computer programs allow students to use technology to help them work with language. Computers can be used in conjunction with writing programs to allow students to type stories. Some computer reading programs, such as Wiggle Works, allow a child to click on a word, and the computer will say the word. Students can also record their voices while reading a story and then play it back listening to the story. This is also a good program for ESL children and children with LD, who may have an auditory preference (students who learn best by hearing words, stories, etc.).

Recorded books, audiotapes to accompany written text, offer another approach. Students listen to the story while they read along with the text. These are very good for students in upper grades, who listen to the story and then complete assignments. Another strategy used by teachers is to record their own stories while they read to the class each day. Following the completion of the book the teacher has an audio recording that can be labeled with a color code or numbering system that corresponds to the book. Students like to listen to recorded books made by their teachers.

Think, Talk, Write/Draw

Personal journals are used by most teachers, and many of them say, by the middle of the week, students have written very little or state that they have nothing to say. One strategy that I developed while working with second-grade students is "Think, Talk, Write." I like to use this with journals on Mondays and Fridays. On Fridays, students are asked to think about what they might do on the weekend. (I give them about one minute.) Next, I have each student turn to someone and tell them what they were thinking, again allowing about one minute. Then, I ask students to write in their journals what they think they might be doing on the weekend. By doing this, students are making predictions. On Monday, I have the students look at what they wrote on Friday (predictions) and repeat the "think, talk" portion. During the talk time, students confirm or reject their Friday predictions. Then, I ask them to write what they actually did based on the new information. "Think, Talk, Write" supports predicting, sampling, and confirming text, which are strategies proficient readers and writers use. The vocabulary students use is more complex (less familiar) because they may be writing about a new experience. Teachers find that surface-level scores reflect a lower spelling accuracy rate because students are using more complex language. This is a good sign. These words can be used as part of the spelling program.

"Think, Talk, Draw" can be used with young children. Follow the same process as above, except ask students to draw a picture of what they might do on the weekend. On Mondays, repeat the process, only this time, have them draw another picture about what they actually did. The emphasis is on the talking and thinking with the drawing acting as a visual representation of their thinking. Sentences can then be added as children develop their writing.

Word Power

In this activity students are given a word such as "encyclopedia" and are asked to use the letters from this word to write other words (e.g., pod, cycle, any, and so on). Students can record their words in a personal dictionary. One fourth-grade class discovered 110 words within the word "encyclopedia." Record the words they come up with on chart paper and keep in an area students can access while writing to check the spelling of certain words. Because students make smaller words from larger ones, the words they generate are "low-frequency" words. Low-frequency words are sometimes referred to as "sight" words, words that teachers feel students need to know how to spell on sight. Word power can be extended to more formal parts of speech (see Figure 5.7).

As students discover words within the long word, they are asked to place them on the chart under the appropriate column. An "Abbreviations" column is included because students quickly become interested in creating a long list, and will often ask if abbreviations can be counted (e.g., the abbreviation "NC" for "North Carolina" is found in "encyclopedia"). Once again, record their words on a large piece of chart paper or on a transparency.

People	Places	Things	Action	Abbreviations

FIGURE 5.7   WORD POWER

Mnemonic Devices

A mnemonic device is a trigger that makes an association between words and spellings that can help one remember seemingly illogical and random spellings. The best mnemonic device is the one you think up for yourself (Phenix & Scott-Dunne, 1991). Here are a few examples:

principal–the princi**pal** is your **pal**
heard–you **hear** with your **ear** and add "d"

Content Areas and Word Study

The following are strategies used to support word study as it relates to content areas.

Social Studies

1. List the continents of the world.
2. List as many cities (in state or province) as you can.
3. Describe the city to a friend.
4. Write the names of the states and their capitals.

Science

1. List as many trees as you can.
2. List insects that begin with a vowel.
3. List as many birds as you can.
4. Can you name an animal or bird that begins with each letter of the alphabet?

Reading

1. List as many books as you can that are found in your room.
2. List the names of as many authors as you can.
3. Survey the class to find out what kinds of books they like to read.
4. Identify characters from books.

English

1. Write the days of the week.
2. List the twelve months of the year.
3. Write a word for each letter of the alphabet.
4. List all of the different languages that you can think of.

Mathematics

1. Think of a number, write it, then create a face from it.
2. Make a list of the students in your class. Beside each name, record the age of the student. Add up the ages using a calculator.
3. Code each letter of the alphabet, starting with the number 1 for the letter "A," number 2 for the letter "B," and so on. Send someone a coded message.
4. Write as many words as you can that have to do with mathematics.

Anything Goes

1. Name things that are made of cloth.
2. Write the names of some movies. Can you classify them (adventure, comedy, mystery, sci-fi)?
3. List as many kinds of sandwiches as you can.
4. List the names of cars.

Summary

Word study represents one-third of an overall writing program. Studying with words helps reveal relationships, patterns, and structures. It is one area students like because they see studying as a game. Word games are fun and help to relax the brain during learning. When a person is relaxed, the brain is able to retain information more successfully. Students who encounter stress "down shift" (Caine & Caine, 1991). When this happens, they look for "safe routes." For instance, they may use words they know how to spell rather than attempting more complex language. Students who use "safe" (more familiar) language are not willing to take risks when they write and spell for fear of being punished. This is why it is important to allow students to write without worrying about the consequences of spelling words wrong.

TEACHER STORY • *Personal Dictionary*

Willie Williams
Grade 7, Social Studies, University Public School
Detroit, Michigan

I wanted my seventh-grade economics class to learn about different vocabulary they would be reading in my class. I did not want to just give them the words and have them look up the definitions in the dictionary, so I gave them the following list of words that they would come across during the semester.

agriculture	deficit	minimum wage
barter	depression	monopoly
bonds	distribution	need
capital	dividend	opportunity cost
capital resource	entrepreneurs	price
capitalism	expenditure	profit
choice	import	recession
circular flow	incentives	resource
command system	macroeconomics	scarcity
commerce	manufacturer	stock
competition	market	supply and demand
consumer	market system	surplus
credit	mercantilism	traditional system
currency		

I gave each one of the students a notebook to compose their own personal dictionary and told them to write their own definitions to these words. Then, as they encountered the words in the textbook, they were to revisit their original definition and compare the two and make the necessary changes. Following is an example from one student's notebook:

Jasmine Porter
Sep. 13, 2001
Third

Economics Glossary

1) agriculture - animals, farming and crop land

2) Barter - the trading of different services

3) Bonds - A form of money you can save for a later time or date

4) Capital - The building in Washington where they pass laws

5) Capitalism - when you own or start your own business

6) Choice - Something that you decide to do.

7) Circular Flow - Something that flows in a circle

8) Command System - a command system

This student wrote a definition for the word "capital" based on her knowledge about the Capitol building in Washington, D.C. As the student learns more about economics, he or she will find that the meaning of the word "capital" changes when it is contextualized. Students are free to ask someone in the class to read their definitions and make suggestions. I collect the notebooks throughout the course of the semester and check the definitions, and then spend time during class asking students to share any definitions they have written with the class. I believe that when students develop their own definitions based on their reading and talking with other students, vocabulary will be more meaningful to them.

6

Genres and Personal Writing

When students are required to write in a variety of genres they learn that certain words are characteristic of those genres. For instance, words used when writing an invitation to a party differ from the words used on a postcard. Students should identify and discuss visual characteristics of a genre before they write. Using the postcard as an example, students should discuss the visual features (a picture on one side, and places to write an address and a short message on the other side) and then try to identify words and phrases they might use that would fit the postcard genre. Imagining everything that they know about postcards enhances their ability to write. Cognitive psychologists refer to this as "activating schemas." Schemas are defined as everything a person knows about a given topic or subject. Before information in our schemas can be used for writing, it has to be activated through talk and discussion. Genres provide students with a variety of formats for writing in all subjects across the curriculum. For instance, a time line can be used in history to track exploration, or in science to follow the development of a cure. A genre approach to writing is not restricted to writer's workshop but can be used across the curriculum.

What Is a Genre?

Writers have options for representing and communicating information, ideas, and stories. For example, poetry offers a range of forms with commonly recognizable features that differ from the features that are used for persuasive writing in narrative form. Each genre presents text in a meaningful way, but differs in how language is used to construct the intended meaning of the text. Each genre includes a variety of writing formats.

What Is a Writing Format?

Writing formats are different forms of writing within a genre with different purposes that address different audiences. Each format is identified through the visual and textual form in which it is presented. For example, the features of an invitation include the way it looks, the purpose it performs (communicating its meaning and message) and the audience it will reach (who will read and respond to it). By examining the features of an invitation, students recognize the differences between it and a postcard.

Students learn how to use written language to communicate by identifying and modeling the visual and textual features of writing formats. As students learn to write in different formats for different purposes and audiences, they learn about the communication potential of language, and they develop their skills as writers.

Purpose and Writing

The purpose for writing varies for each format. Some formats, such as friendly letters and scrapbooks, inform and entertain the reader by providing interesting facts and details in a creative, playful manner. The purpose of other formats include reflecting on events, ideas, or opinions; interpreting something that has been read or an idea that has been developed; explaining how something works or why it works the way it does; providing instructions on how to do something by listing a set of steps; reporting on events that have taken place; or persuading someone into thinking or acting a certain way.

Audience

The audience is the reader(s) who will interpret the text based on its content, its form, and the clarity and focus of its message. Audiences may include classmates, schoolmates, friends, self, parents, teachers, family members, and perhaps the community. Writing for a specific audience makes for stronger, more efficient writing, and affects how the author chooses words, writes sentences, selects drawings and illustrations to include, and chooses the final form in which to share information. Audience selection forces the writer early on to make decisions about the text format.

Visual and Textual Features

What separates writing formats is the unique combination of textual features, language usage, and visual features. Textual features may include, for example, the use of abbreviations and contractions in itineraries, the salutation and closing of a formal letter, the use of dialogue in historical stories, and so on. Visual features may include the five-line form of a cinquain in poetry, the question-and-answer form of an interview, the use of graphics on a poster, and so on. It is important to identify the visual and textual characteristics of formats before students start to write. In so doing, students will be able to organize the semantics and syntax of a piece.

Personal Writing

Many formats on the genre chart can be used for personal writing. In some genres, such as personal journals, students can focus on personal issues without having the work go through revision and editing. The purpose of a learning log is to have students write and reflect on what they have learned about a given topic or subject. A photo essay may involve discussion and planning but does not revision.

Genres and Writing Formats

The genres discussed in this book are structured around eight specific writing formats: personal writing and messages, narrative, poetry, report and inform (informational) writing, traditional literature, word play, instruct and explain writing, and opinion and persuasion writing. These formats were selected because they represent authentic writing experiences which engage students. Each writing format encompasses a range of literary formats (see Figure 6.1). Classroom teachers need to decide which genres and formats suit the goals of the curriculum and work from there.

The writing functions and formats are the kinds of writing that students are likely to be interested in and capable of learning. Using the material students are studying, teachers can create opportunities for writing within these formats. For example, students can write an itinerary for a

Genre	Personal Writing and Messages	Narrative	Poetry	Report and Inform	Traditional Literature	Word Play	Instruct and Explain	Opinion and Persuasion
Formats	• Autobiographies • Diaries • Postcards • Friendly letters • Formal letters • Personal anecdotes • Invitations • Thank-you notes • Itineraries/agendas • Biographical accounts • Learning logs	• Adventure • Mystery • Scripts • Realistic fiction • Science fiction • Historical fiction • Nonfiction	• Rhymes: couplets, quatrains, limericks, lyrics • Patterned poems: cinquains, acrostics, haiku, triads • Free verse: narrative poems	• Time lines • Interviews • Scrapbooks • Surveys • Newspaper articles/headlines • Photo essays/captions • Magazine articles	• Hero tales • Fables • Tall tales • Fairy tales • Folktales • Myths	• Rebuses • Jokes • Riddles • Tongue twisters • Comic strips • Crossword puzzles	• Recipes • Menus • Game rules • Diagrams • Guides • Directions/instructions	• Posters/slogans • Reviews • Advertisements • Brochures • Editorials • Advice/Ask-the-Expert columns • Speeches
Purpose	To inform To explain To reflect To interpret	To entertain To tell a story	To share language as an art form To entertain	To report To inform	To explain To entertain	To entertain	To instruct To explain To guide	To persuade To put forth a point of view
The audience reads to:	Reflect Seek information	Enjoy	Explore language Enjoy	Seek information	Enjoy Seek information	Enjoy	Seek information	Understand another point of view

FIGURE 6.1 *GENRE CHART*

character in a book or story that they are reading, informational diagrams can be included in a magazine article, and a formal letter can be used to request information from a report. In the process of writing, students will learn about the unique textual and visual features embedded in writing formats and how to select formats that support the manner in which they want to communicate.

Personal Writing and Messages (Between You and Me)

Personal writing, such as diaries, journals, and autobiographies, is written for one's self to recount experiences and to reflect on thoughts and feelings. Messages, such as formal letters and itineraries, are sent or shared with other people to provide them with information or to ask them questions. Personal writing and messages give students the opportunity to interpret their thoughts and feelings or to reflect on situations or events occurring around them.

Narrative (What's Your Story?)

Narratives, such as science fiction, historical stories, or personal accounts, use features such as plot, characterization, and setting, allowing students to create a variety of story styles that draw on their imagination, knowledge of history, and life experiences. By exploring and writing narratives, students are given the opportunity to tell stories and to entertain their audiences.

Poetry (Rhythm and Rhyme)

Poetry embraces a variety of styles that include rhyming poems, such as limericks, and narrative poetry. Poetry introduces students to the use of rhyme, rhythm, and pattern and allows them to communicate their ideas and feelings in a creative, entertaining way.

Report and Inform (Get the Scoop!)

Informational writing, such as magazine articles and photo essays, is an interesting way to share facts and information. Exploring informational writing helps students learn how to write about events and issues. It requires students to research facts and to report their findings in an appealing and concise manner.

Traditional Literature (Pass It On)

Traditional literature, such as myths and folktales, is a special type of narrative that entertains and informs readers, often through the presence of a moral or lesson. When students model traditional literature, they extend what they know about narrative styles and can explore and explain their own traditions to their audience. Traditional literature also exposes them to classic retellings of traditional stories.

Word Play (Thought Twisters)

Word play, through such genres as tongue twisters and crossword puzzles, invites students to examine and experiment with language patterns, words, and symbols. They can combine these elements creatively in text to entertain and invite a response from the reader.

Instruct and Explain (Step by Step)

Instructions and explanations, informational diagrams, and guides, are forms of writing that provide helpful information about and guidance through a process. Students write instructions and explanations in order to explain how something is done by following a series of steps or by explaining how or why something works the way it does.

Opinion and Persuasion (Take a Stand)

Persuasive writing is a means for writers to express their opinions. Often, as with editorials, speeches, and advice columns, the writers are also trying to convince someone to think or act in a particular manner, to accept a certain idea, or to follow a piece of advice. Experimenting with persuasive writing encourages students to use convincing language to get across their points of view.

Who Are the Writers?

As students grow and develop physically, emotionally, and cognitively they go through a range of emotions and experiences. The social nature of learning plays an important role in development. This is a time filled with establishing friendships, discovering new ways of learning, and exploring role playing. Students learn about themselves by communicating with family members, with the teacher, with classmates, and with their friends.

Writing As a Developmental Process

A range of writers (like spellers) exists in every classroom. By identifying the characteristics of reluctant, developing, and independent writers teachers are in a better position to help students develop their writing potential. A point of clarification: It should not be assumed that any one type of writer/speller is better or more advanced in their skills than is the other. A writer's/speller's characteristics can change, depending on a number of related issues. The purpose is to use this information as a starting point to move students back and forth along the sliding scale, as no one writer/speller will always be one of the three kinds of writers all of the time.

Depending on their experience with different formats, students may be independent writers one day and reluctant the next. Interest and prior knowledge of a subject often contributes to how well a student can write. For instance, a student who likes sports and wants to write about his or her favorite hockey player in a magazine article may be identified as an independent writer because he or she knows a lot about the subject and will probably write a great deal on the topic. On the other hand, the same student might have a limited knowledge of myths and could be considered to be a developing writer in this format. It is important that students not be identified as just one type of writer but rather as writers with the potential of being any one of the three types.

Reluctant Writers

Reluctant writers do not take risks in their writing. They prefer to use high-frequency words (words they already know how to spell) when they write; as a result, they have very few invented spellings in their drafts. Reluctant writers tend to write only one draft because they are so careful initially. They often write in the first person; for example, while telling a sequence of the events from a day, they would probably use wording such as, "I did this. I did that."

Sliding Scale

← —————————————————————————————————————— →

Reluctant Writers   **Developing Writers**   **Independent Writers**

Characteristics of Reluctant Writers

Reluctant writers share a number of characteristics. They

- have difficulty starting to write.
- focus on accurate spelling (they try few functional spellings).
- ask how to spell a word before writing it.
- use high-frequency words.
- write in the first person.
- write about actual events, often a sequence of events in a day.
- use a limited, unimaginative vocabulary, though they may at times write lengthy stories.
- may not be able to (or want to) find a topic.
- are reluctant to ask for help with ideas from the teacher or their peers.
- tend to do just one draft.
- avoid revising and editing to make their writing better.

Figure 6.2 is a sample of writing by a reluctant writer.

> I wold like to win the Stanly Cup. There my hockey team will be chapons. I love Hockey. My team is going to the cup.

FIGURE 6.2   *RELUCTANT WRITER.* The brevity of this piece indicates that the student has difficulty developing ideas. The writer relies on safe language. Despite short choppy sentences, this piece reflects a basic understanding of punctuation and grammar.

Teaching Strategies to Use with Reluctant Writers

Reluctant writers need to be encouraged to use more complex language and to take risks. They need to break away from the comfort zone that known words provide and to place less emphasis on spelling in their drafts.

- Provide students with resources that are easy to locate in the classroom, such as word lists, personal and group-generated dictionaries, and models or samples of writing displayed in the room.

- Encourage students to do 10 minutes of free writing at the beginning of each writing session to loosen up and let ideas flow.

- Offer students plenty of choices for their writing activities.

- Invite students to read and enjoy examples of the format they want to write in so they have models for their own writing.

- Take time to discuss their topics with them before students begin writing.

- Help the students use charts and webs to develop ideas while they are writing.

- Encourage students to get feedback from independent writers in the classroom; this can stimulate reluctant writers and help them to model what other students are doing.

- Help reluctant writers to go beyond the first draft and into editing and revision.

- Have regular writing conferences to monitor their writing progress. Keep conferences short and ask questions about their writing rather than just provide them with feedback. Use open-ended questions that extend their thinking:

  Why did you choose this topic?
  What do you like about what you have written?
  What will your next step be?
  Are there any other characters you could introduce?
  What kinds of things would they say to each other?
  Do you have a beginning, a middle, and an end?

Open-ended questions lead reluctant writers to consider new or different aspects of their writing. Reluctant writers need to take ownership of their writing by conferring with their peers and making use of available resources, such as lists, models, samples, and so on. When revising and editing their work, these students should be encouraged to go back through their writing and incorporate wishes and other suggestions made by listening editors to make their writing more interesting.

Developing Writers

Developing writers enjoy writing, but they often use vague language and their writing lacks detail. They understand and accept drafts as part of the authoring cycle, and can revise and edit to improve their writing through conferring with others.

Characteristics of Developing Writers

Developing writers share a number of characteristics. They

- can write a first draft on their own.
- use functional spelling when attempting to write unknown words.
- feel comfortable asking others for help.
- write in a way that reflects a basic understanding of grammar and punctuation (by use of capitals, punctuation, and grammar).
- join their thoughts together using connectors, such as "and," "then," and "but."
- have a limited ability to self-edit.
- use resources, such as word lists, word walls, and other textual information as guides.
- tend to use vague language.
- include few details in their writing.
- use a lot of common nouns rather than appropriate proper nouns.

    Figure 6.3 is a sample of writing by a developing writer.

Teaching Strategies to Use with Developing Writers

Developing writers can improve their writing by clarifying and expanding on their ideas.

- Encourage these students to read their drafts with listening editors to get ideas for expanding on the content of and detail in their writing.

> *I personally thought the book was great, and it had great illustrated pictures to. I really really liked Jeoreena or as her friend call her Zip because she saved the kids on the bus, because she knew how to snowshoe and if she didn't who would save them.*

FIGURE 6.3 *DEVELOPING WRITER.* The student uses a variety of sentence structures and demonstrates a basic understanding of punctuation and grammar. However, the writing lacks detail and shows a reliance on safe spellings. The run-on final sentence makes the piece difficult to follow.

- Invite them to record their work on audiotapes; listening to these tapes may assist them in the self-editing and revision process.

- Encourage students to substitute proper nouns for common nouns when they revise their writing. (For example, "my friend's house" can be rewritten using the name of the friend.)

Developing writers need to fine-tune the content of their writing by giving more attention to details when revising sections that are vague or confusing. They have difficulty self-editing for content and need help finding the parts of their stories that need to be revised. Peer editing can help these students decide which sections need clarifying.

Independent Writers

Independent writers are avid writers who can generate new ideas easily. They are risk takers who experiment with language. They understand the writing process and are frequently called upon to act as editors by other students.

Characteristics of Independent Writers

Independent writers share a number of characteristics. They

- initiate writing on their own.
- can generate new ideas easily.
- produce writing that is creative, funny, or exciting.
- include dialogue.
- have a good sense of characterization, plot, and setting.
- feel comfortable using functional spellings.
- like to confer with others about their work.
- can self-edit and revise their writing.
- are often called on to help their peers revise and edit.
- are viewed by their peers as being "experts."
- use a variety of resources to check for accuracy when writing.
- write in a way that is clear and easy to follow.
- accept suggestions from others and incorporate these ideas into their drafts.
- read a wide range of literature.

  Figure 6.4 is a sample of writing by an independent writer.

Teaching Strategies to Use with Independent Writers

Independent writers are self-motivated and enjoy challenges.

- Ask these students questions about their writing to encourage deeper thinking.
- Draw their attention to a variety of literary forms, such as similes, metaphors, and personification, and invite them to use these forms.
- Invite students to compare their writing with that of other authors so they can gather a variety of alternative perspectives.
- Draw their attention to some well-crafted models of literary formats.
- Encourage them to make good use of peer writing conferences to edit and revise their work.

The book is called The Ghost of
Lunenberg Manor. This book kept
me in suspense. I was anxious to
read the next chapter. There was
a brother and a sister. Their names
were Liz and Tom Austen. They were always
trying to help the cops solve
mysterys until they had to solve
a close friends murder mystery.
They miot one clue. They get caught by
the yancks by a horrible man
until a hero comes to their rescue.
They were glad they were back to
normal.

FIGURE 6.4 *INDEPENDENT WRITER.* The writer is comfortable using functional spelling and demonstrates a working knowledge of grammar and punctuation. The writing is clear and easy to follow, with some confusion of word tense. The idea is well developed and displays sequence and logical order.

- Suggest that they experiment with writing in a variety of formats and to try using formats they haven't attempted before.

Independent writers can benefit from working with developing and reluctant writers. While helping others to solve writing problems using a social and collaborative approach, they are challenged to use what they know about language and to solidify their own knowledge of writing.

ESL Writers

ESL writers face special challenges. These students may be independent writers in their first language but may still not fit the descriptions of the reluctant, developing, or independent writer when writing in English. They may have highly developed thought processes but be unable to express their ideas when writing in English.

Teaching Strategies to Use with ESL Writers

ESL writers should be part of the writing classroom and be encouraged to take an active role in writing activities.

- Use pictures, illustrations, and other key visuals to initiate discussions.
- Provide them with a variety of textual sources in the classroom, such as illustrated charts, lists, picture dictionaries, and so on.
- Encourage them to build their own personal dictionary of words. They might add illustrations to help them understand and remember the words.
- Put labels on areas and items in the classroom to help these students connect the location or object to the word.
- Encourage these students to learn about language by talking and listening in groups and by working on activities with peers.
- Set them up with reading/writing buddies who can be a good resource for them. (For example, a partner can transcribe a piece of writing for an ESL writer as they dictate it.)
- Foster good writing and speaking by suggesting that they listen to books read by another person or on audiotapes to hear the rhythm and flow of language.
- Invite them to dictate their stories, poems, and so on into a tape recorder and arrange for parent volunteers to transcribe these onto a computer. Students can then practice reading their own writing.

Writers with Learning Disabilities

Students who have been identified as "exceptional" learners (behaviorally, physically, and mentally challenged students, and students with learning disabilities) may need a modified program with more structure, guidance, and monitoring to meet their needs as writers. These students need to feel that they are a part of the learning environment and should be treated the same as any other class member when groups are assigned. Like all students, they need to understand what the expectations for writing are and to feel that they are a part of the community of writers.

Teaching Strategies with Special Needs Writers

Special needs writers require structured guidance and monitoring to achieve success in a writing program.

- Give these students more structured writing assignments.

- Set short-term, achievable goals for them during conferences.

- Monitor their frustration levels when they're writing and suggest they take short breaks.

- Give them positive feedback regularly.

Writers of all levels of ability improve over time. Look for changes in the content, form, and mechanics of students' writing as they write in different formats. You might observe that some students start using punctuation correctly or that their spellings of certain words are no longer invented. Record these changes as you observe them. Students participate in this kind of evaluation by reflecting on what they have learned and what changes they notice about their own writing.

Setting Up a Framework for Your Writing Program

Students need a classroom framework that supports their development as writers. A framework allows them to function as a community of writers and should consist of

- Rules and expectations
- Writing folders

- Routines
- Portfolios

- Schedules

Having a framework makes everyone aware of what is required of them in the classroom environment. Ensure that all students understand the framework and refer to it often to remind them of their responsibilities during the writing process.

Rules and Expectations

Writing classrooms are busy and active places. When students write, they need to be able to share and discuss their work with others. Rules, expectations, and routines should be established before students are given the freedom of the classroom, and students should be involved in establishing theses rules. When you involve students in the setting of writing expectations, they take ownership of the writing environment. Start by putting the title, "Rules and Expectations" at the top of a chart and ask students for suggestions that apply to the writing process. Some of the responses might include:

- Be patient with others and wait my turn.

- Try to solve my problems before asking for help.

- Help others when asked.

- Edit and revise my own work to the best of my ability.

- Ask a listening editor for advice or an opinion after I have tried to edit my own work.

- Use a quiet voice and respect the learning of others.

- Don't disturb or distract others.

- Accept that mistakes are okay.

- Cooperate during peer conferences and editing.

It's not practical to list all of the rules and expectations on the first day, but when problems arise, draw the students' attention to them and to finding a way to resolve them. Add the solutions to these problems to the list of rules and expectations during the first few months of school.

Not all disruptions are problems. For instance, a student or group of students might discover a new way to revise or edit a piece of work or a better way to work together as a group. Take time to read and review the class rules and expectations with the students occasionally. This reminds them that everyone needs to take an active role in establishing and maintaining a cooperative working environment.

Routines

Students need routines; they like to know the writing schedule, the layout of the classroom, and the location of materials, writing folders, and portfolios. Ensure that students know where all writing materials—pencils, pens, erasers, paper, and so on—are kept and that all unused materials are returned to the proper storage bin, can, box, or shelf after use. Establish routines from the start of the school year.

Do not assume students will know about the authoring cycle. Using the outline in Chapter 4, initiate the authoring cycle at the start of the school year. Once you feel students have a working knowledge of editing and revision and their role as listening and conventional editors you can introduce them to genre functions and formats.

Schedules

Schedule large blocks of time to accommodate the authoring cycle. Students need to write drafts, share their work with other students, revise and edit it, and publish it (perhaps using a computer), which may involve preparing illustrations. They also need time to read to find models for their writing. Set aside an hour to an hour and a half every day, or three days a week in the morning or the afternoon, for students to work on their writing. An integrated approach to the writing process allows students to write during time set aside for other subject areas. Many of the formats have cross-curricular links and can be adapted for use in other subjects. Time lines, articles, and autobiographies, for example, could be used in social studies and science.

Writing Folders

Students need a place to store their writing; writing folders are a simple way to organize this work. They might also contain computer disks, student-recorded audiotapes, or drawings and illustrations. Commercially produced writing folders can be purchased or students can make their own folders out of construction paper or by stapling together standard file folders and decorating them. Establish a location in the room for storing writing folders and decide how they will be organized and distributed. They might be kept on a shelf, in a filing cabinet, or in a file box with hanging folders.

Portfolios

Use portfolios to monitor students' development by collecting samples, referred to as "artifacts," of their work. (Keep samples from all subject areas in students' portfolios.) These portfolios follow students through the grades and show their development in writing and other areas of the curriculum. Writing samples in a portfolio might include a

- published piece of writing.
- drawing or illustration.

- computer disk of student work.

- draft of a format in revision.

Not all work that goes into a portfolio should be completed work, and not all completed work should go into the portfolio. The purpose of the portfolio is to demonstrate a learning profile of the student. Together with each student, choose pieces of work that are representative of the student's learning. Every sample that goes into the portfolio should be date-stamped and have a portfolio reflection card completed by the student attached to it. The reflection card identifies what the sample is, why it was chosen, and what the student learned from working on the selected piece of writing.

Grouping

At different times, students may write alone, with a partner, or in a small, collaborative group. Writing begins as a personal event; students develop their own ideas about which to write. Throughout the writing process, students move from writing alone to sharing with peers to working in a group for input. This movement back and forth from solitary to group work is necessary for students so they can reflect, reconsider, and ask questions of themselves and others in order to improve their writing.

Working with a partner may involve two students who have chosen to write in the same format in collaboration. They could begin by reading samples of the format from the classroom library, or the school resource center (e.g., *The Jolly Postman*) before writing letters. They can use one another as resources, reading and discussing material and using it as a guide for their own writing.

Writing in a group allows students to help one another to develop their writing: The act of writing can be a collaborative process. Students must learn to rely on peers, teachers, and other adults to help them solve problems they encounter during writing, and to get advice and positive feedback.

Conferences

Guiding students through revision and editing naturally includes discussion of their writing. Conferences between teacher and student or between students can involve reading, providing and receiving feedback, and rereading of texts.

Peer Conferences

Encourage students to hold writing conferences with one another for the purpose of revising the content and accuracy of their texts. One student can share his or her text with another student who acts as an "editor" and offer suggestions about improving or clarifying it. The editor's job varies, but peer editors should concentrate on ideas, sequence, plot, characterization, whether there is an opening, middle, and end, and so on. The editor's job is to listen for parts of the text that sound confusing or need clarification. For instance, many students at this age think and write using common nouns (dog, brother, mother, uncle, school, and so on). Peer editors can suggest that proper nouns be used to make the story easier to follow for the reader. At final draft, the editor's job will change to that of proofreader—helping to check the writer's spelling, grammar, and punctuation.

Peer conferences can be set up by a student asking one or more other students in the room for help during semantic revising. An area of the room could be designated as the conference area, where students who need help or are ready for input can meet with other students who are available. Limitations may be needed on the number of students in the conference area at any one time.

Teacher-Student Conferences

Teacher-student conferences provide you with an opportunity to meet with students, read what they are working on, and discuss their writing with them. Some students may need a minilesson on a particular aspect of language, like capitalization. Or, when a student appears to be experiencing "writer's block" or when he or she can't achieve satisfaction from a peer conference, your guidance may be needed with a particular problem. Have this form of conference during scheduled writing time. One-to-one conferences with individual students may be necessary, or with small groups involving three or four students. It is important that other students not disturb the process. This is a time when the teacher and the individual student or small group shouldn't be interrupted. If student have questions they can ask someone else or wait until the conference is over to talk with the teacher.

Conferences with the Struggling Writer

Writer's block is something that students may experience from time to time, when they encounter difficulty finding something to write about or completing what they have begun. If this occurs, students may need individual conferences to help sort out the problems they are experiencing. Many students can talk themselves through a problem during a conference.

Students may develop a lack of interest in what they are writing if they feel that the format or idea they have chosen has lost its appeal or is difficult to write in or about. Assess each situation and decide whether the student should select a new format or idea, have a conference with you or a peer, or continue with the selected format or idea. Rather than discard the work already completed, suggest that the student put the piece in his or her writing folder and revisit it later.

Minilessons

Minilessons are direct instructional lessons about a particular spelling, language usage, or concept. They can be presented as a formal lesson to the whole class, more informally to a small group of students, or to an individual who needs to review a skill or concept. The most effective minilessons come from observations you have made about your students' writing. For example, if several of the students are using connectors such as "then" and "but," rather than ending the sentence, conduct a minilesson on how to begin and end a sentence.

Use observations made during writing conferences and discussions about writing to identify those concepts students have not yet learned. Keeping track of the minilessons provides information when reporting to parents.

Reading and Writing Connection

Reading and writing are complementary processes. Students must be encouraged to write in response to their reading and to read to find models for their writing. In so doing, they will develop, rethink, and shape their ideas into a reasonable form to communicate meaningfully with their intended audience.

Graves (1994) comments that, "It is helpful if students read in the same genre (format) in which they write in order to learn from other writers. . . . We need to show students how to read these texts. . . . Try not to combine reading/writing time into one block . . . , above all, do not try to separate the processes." Students need to read or hear good literature read so that they can use it as a model for their own writing. Reading allows students to identify the unique textual features of different formats. This helps them to understand that writing has many different formats and that each format has a specific purpose.

Classroom Writing Strategies

The following classroom writing strategies are intended to help students develop writing skills. Unlike writing for publication, classroom writing strategies are personal and do not require revision and editing. They are intended to allow students an opportunity to use writing to communicate.

Message Boards

Message "boards" are places where students can leave messages for others students, or the teacher can leave messages for students. Apple-juice cans work well because they can be taped together and fit nicely together on a shelf. Students are given time during the day to write a note to another student and place the note in the message board. Time is given for students to read the notes and write a response. Teachers also use the message board for notices and memos that need to go home.

Written Conversation

Written conversation is having a discussion on paper. Two students write together on one piece of paper. To start, one student writes a question to the other student. The question is open-ended and can be about anything. When the student is done he or she passes the paper to his or her partner, who reads the question, starts a new line, and writes an answer. Following the written answer, the same student writes a question back to his or her partner. The paper is passed back to the partner and the process is repeated (partner writes an answer and a question). Teachers can focus the conversation by having students take the role of, say, two characters in a story who are talking. Teachers can introduce this strategy to parents and suggest they have a written conversation at home with their children.

Learning Logs

Learning logs are used to allow students to write about concepts and topics they are learning in different subjects. For instance, students may be asked to write what they learned about geometric shapes in mathematics, amphibians in science. They might explain what they know about dinosaurs or what a polar cap is in geography.

Assessing Writing

Assessing student writing should be the responsibility of the student as well as the teacher. The following are strategies teachers can use to shift the focus of assessment from teachers to students. Because assessment is viewed as a kind of reflection, the strategies suggested are intended to give students an opportunity to think about what they liked about their writing as well as those things that need more attention.

Individual Writing Tracking Sheet

Students use this strategy (see Figure 6.5) to keep track of the genre and format they are working on.

Writing Comment Sheet

This assessment (see Figure 6.6) is used when students have completed publishing a particular writing format. It provides an opportunity for the student and the teacher to reflect and record comments.

As part of their reflection on their writing students can evaluate their work (see Figure 6.7), identifying what they thought worked for them and what they think they should work on more. They are also asked to give advice to other students who may want to engage in this type of writing.

Portfolios are popular with many teachers. A portfolio reflection card (see Figure 6.8) can be used to help students think about their writing. They complete the card, attach it to their writing piece and place it in their portfolios.

Summary

During the reading and writing process, students also listen and speak. For example, during peer writing conferences, asking questions of the authors leads them to consider new information. Talking clarifies situations involving confusing text and may lead an author to make changes to the content of a piece of writing. The classroom environment provides opportunities for students not only to read and write in different formats but also to be able to discuss, share, revise, and edit their work in a collaborative and social setting.

Individual Writing Tracking Sheet

Name: _____

F = First Draft
R = Revising/Editing
FD = Final Draft

Date	Format	Status	Comments

FIGURE 6.5 *INDIVIDUAL WRITING TRACKING SHEET*

Source: From *Writing Sense: Your Writing Skills Handbook, Level 6,* by Gerald R. Oglan. Copyright © 1997 Harcourt Canada. Reprinted with permission.

Writing Comment Sheet

Name: _____

Format	Date	Student's Comments	Teacher's Comments

FIGURE 6.6 *WRITING COMMENT SHEET*

Source: From *Writing Sense: Your Writing Skills Handbook, Level 6,* by Gerald R. Oglan. Copyright © 1997 Harcourt Canada. Reprinted with permission.

Evaluation of _____ (Format)

Name: _____ Date: _____

I have just finished writing a _____ (format).

Before I tried this type of writing, I read: _____
_____

Three things I liked about this type of writing: _____

1) _____

2) _____

3) _____

One thing I found difficult about this type of writing: _____
_____

What I would do differently next time: _____
_____

Advice I would give to a classmate: _____
_____

I had a writing conference with _____

We talked about _____
_____

My peer editor was _____

We worked together by _____
_____

I went through these stages of the writing process: (Check them off.)

❑ Outline   ❑ Revising   ❑ Editing   ❑ Final Draft

❑ First Draft   ❑ Second Draft   ❑ Proofreading   ❑ Publishing

---

FIGURE 6.7   *EVALUATION OF* _____ *(FORMAT)*

Source: From *Writing Sense: Your Writing Skills Handbook, Level 6,* by Gerald R. Oglan. Copyright © 1997 Harcourt Canada. Reprinted with permission.

Portfolio Reflection Card

Name: _____

Date: _____

Format: _____

I am adding this piece of writing to my portfolio because …

_____

_____

_____

_____

FIGURE 6.8   *PORTFOLIO REFLECTION CARD*

Source: From *Writing Sense: Your Writing Skills Handbook, Level 6,* by Gerald R. Oglan. Copyright © 1997 Harcourt Canada. Reprinted with permission.

TEACHER STORY • *Traveling Journals*

Rhonda Calloway
Grade 7, University Public School
Detroit, Michigan

I use Traveling Journals in conjunction with D.E.A.R (Drop Everything And Read). I keep books in the classroom that are considered classics, such as *Around the World in Eighty Days,* books by Mark Twain, and so on, and tell the students that once they finish a book they can fill out a traveling journal sheet (see Figure 6.9).

Traveling Journal

Dear Student,

Once you have finished reading a book, rate it on a scale from 1–10. A score of 1 means you did not like the book at all, while a score of 10 means that you really liked the book and would recommend it to other students to read.

Place the score in the rating box and then tell why you gave it that score. Read what other classmates had to say about the book and agree or disagree with them and tell why. Use the back of this page to write your comments.

Happy Reading.

Book: *Around The World In 80 Days*
Author: *Jules Verne*
Name: *Janelle Moore*
School: *University Public School*
Date: *9/14/01*   Rating

10

FIGURE 6.9 *TRAVELING JOURNAL*

Students rate the book on a scale of 1 to 10 with 1 being a low rating and 10 being the highest rating. Once students rate the book, they have to explain why they gave it the rating that they did.

> I gave this book a 10 because I like to travel. This book takes me all over the world. It is very intresting I'd recommend this book to people who enjoy action and traveling.

Journal sheets are then placed in a binder with other rating sheets. Students from the class can refer to the sheets before deciding to read a certain book. Also, because I have more than one language arts class, students from other classes can read the sheets or compare their ratings against others. Students love the traveling journal and when they finish reading a book and complete a journal sheet their names are written on a bookmarker, which is placed on the wall (see Figure 6.10).

FIGURE 6.10   *TRAVELING JOURNAL BOOKMARKER*

7

Where to Begin?

Assessing the Classroom Writing Program

You will find it helpful to write in all of the strategies used in your classroom on the communication chart (see Figure 7.1). This serves as a "gap analysis" and provides a starting point. As more strategies are used, add them to the chart. It may be useful to write in assessment strategies as well. For instance, if running records or cloze assessments were used, then include them on the chart. Having a working knowledge of the cueing systems helps when making decisions about which systems students are using as they read, write, speak, listen, view, and represent information.

Tracking students' written work is another program area to assess. Whether portfolios, writing folders, or both are used, some way of collecting and tracking writing over the course of the year is needed. In 1998, the National Assessment of Educational Progress (Reading Teacher, 2000) published Writing Assessment results that highlighted the following statistics:

- 75 to 81 percent of students in grades 4, 8, and 12 who reported that they or their teachers saved their work in portfolios scored higher than those who did not.

- 47 percent of fourth-graders, 66 percent of eighth-graders, and 67 percent of twelfth-grade students who reported that their teachers expected them to plan for writing scored higher than students who said they were not expected to plan.

	Reading	Writing	Speaking	Listening	Viewing	Representing
Semantics	photo survey, webs/Maps, brainstorming, Think Aloud, cloze text, DRTA, Interviews/Questionaires	brainstorming, KWL, storyline, Semantic writing, journal writing, auth. chair, cloze, dictations, rubric	role play, debating, Conversation, sports/newscasting, presentations, singing, rehearsal, discussion of sub area, KWL- knowledge of sub area, *Think, talk, write*	storytelling, conversation, discussion, following directions, retelling, Audio tapes, books on tape, pattern books	brainstorming, discussion, computers, game boys, video taping, story boards, wordless books +	diorama, sculpture/painting, drawing/painting, videos, posters, acting, KWL, basic illustrations
Syntax	journals, creative writing, cloze, Shared Reading Survey, Self Corr., newspapers	cloze, journals, Sum. Sequence, Rubrics, Venn diagrams/webs, Maps, dictations, pattern books, shared writing	role play, debate, conversation, Sports newscasts, presentations, singing, writing notes/outlines, using graphic organizers, *retelling	storytelling, music, following directions, pattern books, dictations	Computers, game boys, diorama, ordering pics., cartoons	poetry/raps, music, maps/webs, videos, posters, acting
Graphophonemics	Inv. Spelling, cloze, Shared rebus, writing their own, Read-aloud Checklist	Journal writing, creative writing/Editing, tracker models, Rubric, Spelling Analysis, Venn diagrams/webs, Maps, Think, Talk, Write	sports newscasts, presentations, singing, taking notes, research, making visuals, taps/cds, Shared reading survey	storytelling, following directions, Shared Reading Survey	Computers, game boys, Rebus Stories, Lite performances, skits	music, posters, Kinesthetics, webs/Maps
Pragmatics	book rating rubric, self-editing/corr., predicting, newspapers, Reading Survey, Interest Survey, Recycled Stories, Interviews	Problem solving ?s, poetry writing, making lists, response journal, word hunts, Venn diagrams/webs, Maps, Think, Talk, Write, Draw	Retelling, KWL, role playing, debating, singing, organ/speech or lecture	storytelling, conversation, following directions, Retelling, dictations	Sharing, discussions, video, computers, drawing on a specific, idea, learning logs, Art, drama/skits	Venn diagrams/webs, videos, music, posters, acting in character, manipulatives, story boards, illustrations, Maps

FIGURE 7.1   SAMPLE COMMUNICATION CHART

- Over 80 percent of students in all three grades who said their teachers asked them to do multiple drafts of writing scored higher.

- Over 80 percent of students who said their teachers always or sometimes talked with them about their writing scored higher.

- At least two-thirds of students at all three grade levels who said they discussed their studies with someone at home at least once a week recorded higher-than-average scores.

These statistics bear out my experience that students who plan for writing, talk about their writing, keep track of and collect samples of their writing, and share their work with others score higher on writing tests.

Assessing Writing and Spelling

By observing children as they write and talking with them about their writing, teachers are in a better position to make informed curricular decisions. The following list serves as a guideline of what to look for when observing children and evaluating their writing.

Student Evaluation K–3

- Symbols to letters
- Segmentation (spacing)
- Use of punctuation
- Transition from upper case to lower case
- Patterns and spelling strategies
- Overgeneralizations
- When in doubt ask the child.

Keeping in mind the developmental nature of spelling, discussed in Chapter 2, helps in monitoring a child's writing growth over time.

In working with older students look for the following:

Student Evaluation 4–8

- Safe spellings
- One-letter misses and transpositional spellings
- Surface-level edits
- Spelling strategies
- The use of patterns

In assessing a student's writing, involve the student whenever possible. Students should reflect about their writing. This can be done on a reflection card attached to the writing. On it, the student can explain what they liked about the piece and what changes they would make or what recommendations they would offer to a classmate who was about to write in the same genre.

Goal Setting

Students should be expected to set monthly goals (see Figure 7.2) for themselves in writing and spelling. For instance, they may set a goal that relates to working on endings for stories or transitions from paragraph to paragraph. They may set a goal to write more expository text or work more at semantic editing and revision. Each month students should be given time to read and comment on their goals and set new goals for the next month. The following is a monthly goal form teachers can use with students.

Assessing for Writer's Workshop

Setting up the writer's workshop involves "taking stock" of your classroom environment. Is the classroom set up for editing and revision? Is there space for an editor's table? Are there plenty of reference materials for students to use? Students should be involved in establishing the classroom rules and routines. These should be posted. Discuss the tracking sheet with the students so they know they will be monitored during writer's workshop.

Writer's Workshop

Establish a program plan that addresses word study, personal writing, and writing for publication. Large blocks of time are recommended for writer's workshop. A rule of thumb is 45 to 60 minutes, twice a week. However, scheduling may vary, depending on the class and timetable issues.

The strategies for initiating revision and editing are key to shifting the focus from the teacher to the student. Semantic editing by itself, without initiating a full writing program, will be beneficial to students. Many performance-based tests (like the Michigan Educational Assessment Profile and the provincewide testing in Ontario, Canada) require students to initiate a piece of writing and take it through the steps of the writing process. Two areas that pose the greatest challenges for students on these types of tests are editing and revision. Having students work on revision

Writing Goals for the Month (or Theme)

Name: _____ Date: _____

I am already good at these types of writing: _____

_____

_____

I would like to try these types of writing this month:

_____

_____

I need to work on these things in all my writing:

(ideas, characters, plot, dialogue, using new words, spelling, punctuation,

grammar) _____

_____

_____

_____

I need to work on these stages of the writing process: (Check them off.)

   ❑ Outline   ❑ Revising   ❑ Editing   ❑ Final Draft

   ❑ First Draft ❑ Second Draft ❑ Proofreading ❑ Publishing

I want to try more work ❑ independently

                    ❑ with a partner

                    ❑ with a group

I would like to have writing conferences with

1) _____ about _____

2) _____ about _____

3) _____ about _____

FIGURE 7.2 *WRITING GOALS FOR THE MONTH (OR THEME)*

Source: From *Writing Sense: Your Writing Skills Handbook, Level 6,* by Gerald R. Oglan. Copyright © 1997 Harcourt Canada. Reprinted with permission.

using stories similar to the ones they write will give them an edge when they are expected to write on the annual testing.

Parents, Writing, and Spelling

The standards developed by the International Reading Association/ National Council of Teachers of English (IRA/NCTE) are stated as:

> The responsibility for parental involvement lies on both parents and schools. Parents must seek ways to become involved, and schools must organize to include parents in their assessments and staff development programs, and actively seek their participation. . . . Involving parents in the assessment process includes involving them in staff development or community learning projects in which they learn more about reading and writing. It also includes the use of communication and reporting procedures between schools and home that enable parents to talk in productive ways with their children about their reading and writing. Involving parents and parent communities in the development of new reporting procedures is essential, since they are the primary audience for such reports. (p. 38)

Parents often have experienced a different educational system, driven by a traditional, closed model of learning. The education their children are receiving supports an open model of learning. As a result a dilemma exists (Oglan, 1997). The dilemma involves four key areas.

1. Changes in learning theory are not consistent with the learning experiences of parents.

2. Research on learning over the last 15 years has had a profound impact on classroom instruction.

3. Parents have an innate desire to "know."

4. Parents need to develop their "voices."

Changes in Learning Theory

In Chapter 1, I discussed the empirical and interpretive paradigms. The learning experiences of parents can be associated with an empirical paradigm. Parents of this generation of children were brought up on weekly spelling tests and were assessed with letter grades and percentages. Error was viewed as a weakness. Classrooms where rubrics and personal reflection are used for assessment are foreign to these parents. Telling a parent that spellers are no longer used, without providing additional information, is misleading and can lead to misunderstanding. Teachers and schools need to support the IRA/NCTE standards and provide in-services for parents so that they can become part of the learning community. In so doing, schools place parents in a better position to help their children at home and support the programs at school.

Research on Learning

Research on teaching and learning continues to evolve. The interpretive paradigm challenges traditional beliefs about learning. As a result, how children learn to write and read is at the forefront of national debates. Standards, outcomes-based education, and high-stakes testing have become assessment issues. It is hard enough for teachers to stay on top of these issues; parents are at even more of a disadvantage.

Parents Have an Innate Desire to "Know"

As a parent of two children, hardly a day goes by without my wife or myself wanting to know things. For instance, we want to know who they are going to the show with, how they will get there, and what time they will be home. It seems as if our days are filled with questions, and when we do not get answers, we are concerned about safety, health, nutrition, and so on. The same innate desire we possess as parents applies to schooling and the education of our children. When a parent asks a teacher about how to teach spelling and a teacher responds by telling the parent not to worry about invented spelling, that it is part of learning to spell, parents become concerned. Why? To a parent who may have been brought up in another style of educational system, this type of answer is cause for concern. The problem can increase when a well-intentioned teacher does not or cannot explain or take the time to demonstrate to parents how spelling is dealt with in their writing programs. Parents need to know that whatever program a teacher is using will address the needs of their children, thus putting the parent's innate desire to "know" at rest.

Parents Need to Develop Their "Voice"

When parents feel schools are willing to listen and take an interest in their concerns, they are encouraged to get involved with schools on a number of levels. Parents need to have conversations within the school community that are not confrontational in nature but are proactive. Parents whose only experiences with schools are negative or reactive have a hard

Sharing My Writing

Name: _____ Date: _____

Writing Format: _____

Dear Family,

I am bringing home this piece of writing because…

_____

_____

_____

_____

_____

_____

Student Signature _____

Teacher Signature _____

- -

Please write your comments about this piece of writing. I will share them

with my teacher. _____

_____

_____

_____

_____

_____

Signature of Family Member _____

Date _____

FIGURE 7.3 *SHARING MY WRITING*

Source: From *Writing Sense: Your Writing Skills Handbook, Level 6,* by Gerald R. Oglan. Copyright © 1997
Harcourt Canada. Reprinted with permission.

time developing a voice in matters that concern not only them and their children but the school community in general. Schools can help parents develop a voice by encouraging them to run for school councils, and offering workshops about issues they are concerned about, including workshops on writing programs. In addition, they could invite parents to write family stories and take them through the authoring cycle. At the end of the session, they could have an "author's celebration" where parents get to read their stories to other parents. I like to view parents as a part of the learning community. By including parents, we provide support for them as they try to cope with changes to the educational system and with insights and awareness as they work with their children at home.

Parents should be involved with their child's writing and spelling programs. Figure 7.3 can be used with parents to involve them in their child's writing and spelling development.

Summary

Teachers who have embraced the strategies discussed in this book indicate they have changed their writing programs for the better. It may be necessary from time to time throughout the year to revisit the process of revision and conventional editing. It may involve more minilessons. Spelling improves the more a person writes. But writing must be initiated through interest and real-life situations.

Parents need to be kept informed about writing and spelling programs. Send home newsletters or hold an open house to explain your program to parents. Offer parents information on how students develop reading, writing, speaking, and listening skills so they can work with their children at home.

The information offered in this book does not come with a guarantee. You need to commit to the process, knowing that some things may work better than others. Having one other staff member trying similar changes provides an ideal opportunity for dialogue.

References

Allen, J. P. B., & Van Buren, P. (1971). *Chomsky: Selected readings.* New York: Oxford Press.

Atwell, N. (1987). *In the middle: Writing, reading, and learning with adolescents.* Portsmouth, NH: Heinemann.

Bryson, B. (1990). *The mother tongue: English and how it got that way.* New York: Morrow.

Caine, R. N., & Caine, G. (1991). *Making connections: Teaching and the human brain.* Alexandria, VA: Association for Supervision and Curriculum Development.

Calkins, L. (1991). *Living between the lines.* Toronto: Irwin.

Dewey, J. (1938). *Experience and education.* Toronto: Collier MacMillan.

Goodman, K. (1967). Reading: A psycholinguistic guessing game. *Journal of Reading Specialists 6,* 126–135.

Goodman, K. (1996). *Ken Goodman on reading.* Portsmouth, NH: Heinemann.

Goodman, K., Goodman, Y., & Hood, W. (1989). *The whole language evaluation book.* Portsmouth, NH: Heinemann.

Graves, D. H. (1994). *A fresh look at writing.* Portsmouth, NH: Heinemann.

Hall, N. (1987). *The emergence of literacy.* Portsmouth, NH: Heinemann.

Halliday, M. (1977). *Learning how to mean: Explorations in the development of language.* New York: Elseiver.

Harste, J. C., Short, K. G., & Burke, C. (1988). *Creating classrooms for authors.* Portsmouth, NH: Heinemann.

Harste, J. C., Woodward, V. A., & Burke, C. (1984). *Language stories and literacy lessons.* Portsmouth, NH: Heinemann.

IRA/NCTE Joint Task Force on Assessment. (1994). *Standards for the assessment of reading and writing.* Newark, DE, & Urbana, IL: IRA/NCTE.

Kliebard, H. (1989). *The struggle for the American curriculum, 1893–1958.* New York: Routledge, Chapman and Hall.

National Assessment of Educational Report. (2000). *The reading teacher.*

Newman, J. (1984). *The craft of children's writing.* Toronto: Scholastic.

Oglan, G. R., & Elcombe, A. (2001). *Parent to parent: Our children, their literacy.* Urbana, IL: National Council of Teachers of English.

Oglan, G. R., & Donnelly, A. (1999). When you wish upon a story: Teaching revision in the fourth grade. *Language Arts Journal of Michigan.*

Oglan, G. R. (1992). *Spelling: A transactive process.* Doctoral dissertation, University of South Carolina, Columbia.

Oglan, G. R. (1997). *Parents, learning, and whole language classrooms.* Urbana, IL: National Council of Teachers of English.

Oglan, G. R., & Booth, D. (1997). *Writing sense.* Toronto: Harcourt Brace Canada.

Phenix, J., & Scott-Dunne, D. (1991). *Spelling instruction that makes sense.* Markham, Ontario, Canada: Pembroke.

Rice, J. M. (1897). On the futility of the spelling grind. *Forum, 23,* I & II, 163–172, 409–419.

Rosenblatt, L. (1978). *The reader, text, and the poem.* Cambridge, MA: Harvard University Press.

Shephard, G. D., & Regan, W. B. (1982). *Modern elementary curriculum.* New York: Holt, Rinehart and Winston.

Short, K., Harste, J., & Burke, C. (1996). *Creating classrooms for authors and inquirers.* Portsmouth, NH: Heinemann.

Shubert, W. H. (1986). *Curriculum, perspectives, paradigms and possibilities.* London, Ontario, Canada: Collier MacMillan.

Sylwester, R. (1995). *A celebration of neurons: An educator's guide to the human brain.* Alexandria, VA: Association for Supervision and Curriculum Development.

Vygotsky, L. S. (1978). *Mind in society: The development of higher psychological processes.* Cambridge, MA: Harvard University Press.

Weaver, C. (2002). *Reading process and practice: From sociopsycholinguistics to whole language* (3rd ed.). Portsmouth, NH: Heinemann.

Wells, G. (1986). *The meaning makers: Children learning language and using language to learn.* Portsmouth, NH: Heinemann.

Whitin, D., Mills, H., & O'Keefe, T. (1990). *Living and learning mathematics.* Portsmouth, NH: Heinemann.

Zvric, G. (1997). *Exploratory conversations: Talking to learn.* Doctoral dissertation, University of South Carolina, Columbia.

Index